M000169072

IMAGES OF THE
NATIONAL ARCHIVES

COLD WAR

IMAGES OF THE NATIONAL ARCHIVES

COLD WAR

STEPHEN TWIGGE

PEN & SWORD HISTORY

AN IMPRINT OF PEN & SWORD BOOKS LTD.
YORKSHIRE – PHILADELPHIA

First published in Great Britain in 2020 by
The Images of the National Archives
An imprint of
Pen & Sword Books Ltd
Yorkshire - Philadelphia

Copyright © Stephen Twigge, 2020

ISBN 978 1 52673 990 2

The right of Stephen Twigge to be identified as Author of this work has been asserted by him in accordance with the Copyright, Designs and Patents Act 1988.

The National Archives logo device is a trade mark of
The National Archives and is used under licence.

The National Archives logo © Crown Copyright 2018 © Crown Copyright images reproduced by permission of The National Archives, London England, 2018.

The National Archives is the official archives and publisher for the UK Government, and for England and Wales. We work to bring together and secure the future of the public record, both digital and physical, for future generations.

The National Archives is open to all, offering a range of activities and spaces to enjoy, as well as our reading rooms for research. Many of our most popular records are also available online.

A CIP catalogue record for this book is available from the British Library.

All rights reserved. No part of this book may be reproduced or transmitted in any form or by any means, electronic or mechanical including photocopying, recording or by any information storage and retrieval system, without permission from the Publisher in writing.

Typeset in Minion Pro 11/14.5 by
Aura Technology and Software Services, India.

Printed and bound in the UK by CPI Group (UK) Ltd., Croydon, CR0 4YY.

Pen & Sword Books Ltd incorporates the Imprints of Pen & Sword Books Archaeology, Atlas, Aviation, Battleground, Discovery, Family History, History, Maritime, Military, Naval, Politics, Railways, Select, Transport, True Crime, Fiction, Frontline Books, Leo Cooper, Praetorian Press, Seaforth Publishing, Wharncliffe and White Owl.

For a complete list of Pen & Sword titles please contact

PEN & SWORD BOOKS LIMITED
47 Church Street, Barnsley, South Yorkshire, S70 2AS, England
E-mail: enquiries@pen-and-sword.co.uk
Website: www.pen-and-sword.co.uk

or

PEN AND SWORD BOOKS
1950 Lawrence Rd, Havertown, PA 19083, USA
E-mail: Uspen-and-sword@casematepublishers.com
Website: www.penandswordbooks.com

CONTENTS

Operation Antler, UK nuclear test, 1957. *WO 320/3*

INTRODUCTION

The Cold War dominated international relations for the latter half of the twentieth century. From its beginnings in the rubble of a defeated Germany to its end with the collapse of the Soviet Union, the Cold War was a battle of ideology and power politics supported by military might. It pitted the democratic capitalist West against the communist states of Eastern Europe and Asia and resulted in a series of flashpoints that brought the world to the brink of nuclear war. Paradoxically, due to the catastrophic consequences of armed conflict, the Cold War was characterised by a reassuring stability that developed its own internal dynamic marked by an unwritten code of behaviour. Nuclear weapons were developed and deployed in ever growing numbers, their use constrained by the certain oblivion known as mutually assured destruction (MAD). Vast intelligence networks were brought into being to mitigate uncertainty and prevent miscalculation. Intentions and capabilities were carefully calibrated. Local wars were prevented from spreading by a system of political control that allowed the two superpowers to project power on a global scale with proxy wars fought out in the newly independent states of Asia and Africa. The Cold War was punctuated by a succession of international crises, summit meetings and treaty negotiations which marked the ebb and flow of the East West confrontation.

The aim of the book is to chart the evolution of the Cold War from a number of different perspectives. The first chapter examines international diplomacy and the role played by nuclear weapons in this process. The events described include the creation of the United Nations, the consequences of the Marshall Plan on European recovery and the outbreak of the Korean War. Subsequent analysis focusses on the death of Stalin and the beginnings of peaceful co-existence. The dangers of the Cuban missile crisis and Britain's decision to purchase the Polaris missile system are also discussed. The chapter concludes with the Soviet invasion of Afghanistan, the uprisings in Eastern Europe and the collapse of the Soviet Union. Chapter 2 explores the military confrontation between the two superpowers and charts the creation of the two major Cold War military alliances, the North Atlantic Treaty Organisation (NATO) and the Warsaw Pact. The intelligence networks established by both sides is the focus of Chapter 3. The events described include the unmasking of the atomic spies Alan Nunn May and Klaus Fuchs, the significance of the Cambridge and

Portland spy rings and the role played by the Soviet double agents Oleg Penkovsky and Oleg Gordievsky.

The second half of the book concentrates on civil defence, the protest movement, proxy wars in Africa and the popular culture. Chapter 4 illustrates the consequences of nuclear war and assesses the value of civil defence in the nuclear age. The government's plans for fighting and surviving a nuclear war are explored. Details are provided of the wartime bunkers from which the country would be controlled following a nuclear exchange. The protest movement is the theme of Chapter 5 and concentrates on the activities of the Campaign for Nuclear Disarmament (CND) and its more radical offshoots the Committee of 100 and Spies for Peace. The chapter concludes with the establishment of a women's peace camp at Greenham Common in response to the deployment of cruise missiles in the 1980s. Chapter 6 investigates the proxy wars fought in Africa during the Cold War and highlights the various conflicts that took place within the Congo, Angola, Mozambique, Zimbabwe and South Africa. Chapter 7 explores the cultural dimension of the Cold War and examines a variety of books, films and pop songs that reflect the fears and anxieties of growing up in the shadow of the bomb. The final chapter looks forward to the future and outlines the new challenges facing the international community in the twenty-first century. The primary narrative of each chapter is told from a British viewpoint and is based on records held by The National Archives of the United Kingdom at Kew.

Left: **Cartoon depicting the defeat of Nazi Germany by the combined efforts of Britain and the Soviet Union.** *INF 2/31*

Below: **Comrades In Arms poster (Churchill and Stalin) 1939-1945.** *EXT 1/48*

CHAPTER 1

ATOMIC: NUCLEAR WEAPONS AND INTERNATIONAL RELATIONS

On 5 August 1945, the Japanese city of Hiroshima was totally destroyed by an atomic bomb dropped from a B-29 US bomber, the *Enola Gay*. The explosion was the climax of a top secret mission to develop the atomic bomb, known as the Manhattan Project, which had been underway since 1942. Three days later, the city of Nagasaki was obliterated in a second atomic attack. The destruction of the two cities resulted in the death of

Churchill, Truman and Stalin meet to negotiate terms for the end of World War II in Potsdam 26 July 1945. *CO 1069/892*

over 200,000 Japanese civilians and is widely seen as marking the end of the Second World War. Nazi Germany was defeated on 8 May 1945 with Japan announcing its surrender on 15 August 1945. The three victorious powers (the United States, Soviet Union and Britain) met at Potsdam in Germany to agree the post-war world order but soon fell out, with each country seeking to advance its own agenda. The political and destructive power of the atomic bomb heralded the beginning of a new arms race between the liberal democracies of the West led by the United States and the one party system championed by the Soviet Union and its communist allies.

The task of drawing up an agreed set of norms to govern the post-war world and regulate further development of nuclear energy was given to the newly formed United Nations (UN). Established in 1945 by fifty countries, the leaders of the UN had high hopes that the organization would reduce international tension and prevent future conflicts between

Hiroshima after the bomb, August 1945. *AIR 8/1788*

nations spiralling into war. To maintain peace and security, the UN established a Security Council composed of five permanent members (America, Britain, China, France and the Soviet Union) with the authority to sanction peacekeeping operations, enforce international sanctions, and authorize collective military action through resolutions of the Security Council. The first session of the Security Council took place in London on 17 January 1946. The headquarters of the UN including the General Assembly building were later established in 1952 in New York, overlooking the East River.

To prevent the devastation of nuclear war, the UN sought to abolish the possession of atomic weapons by individual states. Future research into atomic energy would be undertaken on a collective basis by an international organization under UN control. The US agreed to dismantle its stockpile and turn over its atomic research on the condition that all other countries pledged never to produce nuclear weapons and agreed to a credible system of inspection. In response, the Soviets demanded the immediate abolition of all nuclear weapons leaving the question of verification to be agreed at a later date. The negotiations at the UN became deadlocked, with each side blaming the other. The failure of international control allowed individual countries to embark on atomic energy programmes of their own, including the development and production of nuclear weapons.

The stalemate in the UN was soon reflected in events on the ground. In Europe, rather than relinquishing its hold over Eastern European countries and allowing free elections, as agreed at the Yalta conference in 1944, the Soviets quickly installed communist regimes friendly to Moscow. Less than three years after the end of the war, Soviet style governments had assumed power in eleven European states with a combined population of over 100 million people. The speed at which the Soviets had managed to expand their political, economic and social system into Eastern Europe began to concern the western powers. The lack of food and resources in the early post war years and the continued need for rationing was exploited by the French, German and Italian communist parties who demanded radical change to the economic and political order. Strikes and industrial unrest soon spread to the major cities. There was growing concern in Washington and London that the democratic institutions of the West could soon be overwhelmed if nothing was done to improve the situation.

One of the first western leaders to recognise the potential danger was Winston Churchill, Britain's wartime Prime Minister, who warned that an 'iron curtain' had descended across Europe and that the states of central and Eastern Europe were now effectively controlled by Moscow. To deter further Soviet expansion, Churchill advocated the creation of a western alliance armed with nuclear weapons. Churchill's concern over the direction of Soviet policy confirmed earlier reports written by Frank Roberts, a senior diplomat stationed at

Yalta conference 1945: Churchill, Stalin and Roosevelt. *INF 14/447*

the British embassy in Moscow. In a series a telegrams sent directly to Ernest Bevin, the Foreign Secretary, Roberts cautioned that Moscow interpreted compromise as a sign of weakness and argued that the time for one sided appeasement and concessions was over. These views echoed similar sentiments expressed by his US counterpart George Keenan, in his famous 'long telegram' which underpinned the policy of containment.

Western concerns over Soviet ambitions were further reinforced in 1948 when Soviet authorities unilaterally suspended all passenger and trade routes into West Berlin, which was still under western military control. Situated 100 miles inside the Soviet zone of occupation and surrounded by Russian troops, West Berlin was isolated and vulnerable

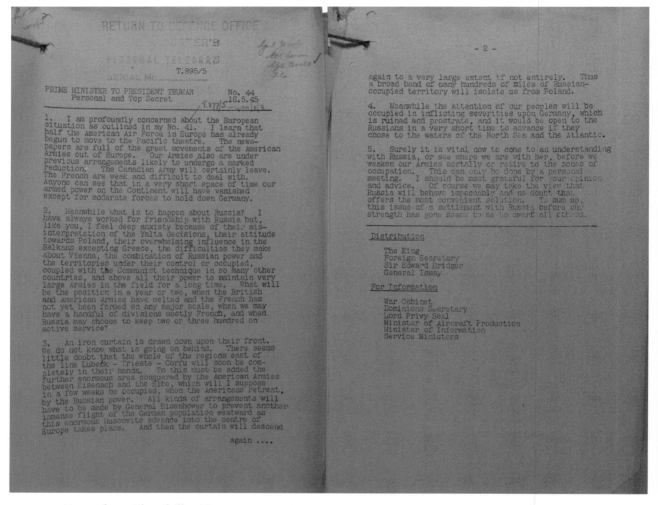

Letter from Churchill to Truman expressing concern over post-war Soviet intentions, May 1945.
CAB 120/186

to Soviet threats. The western allies refused to be bullied out of the city and organised an airlift to supply the besieged citizens of Berlin with food and fuel. Unwilling to provoke the West further and risk armed conflict, the Soviets backed down. To demonstrate its commitment to its western allies, the United States approved the Marshall Plan, which provided $12 billion in aid to sixteen European countries. The transfer of funds helped to rebuild the shattered economies of Western Europe, remove trade barriers and prevent the spread of communism. Moscow refused to participate and prevented its Eastern European satellites from taking part in the scheme. The events of the late 1940s convinced European leaders that the only way to maintain the balance of power in Europe was to

- 5 -

77

From Stettin in the Baltic to Trieste in the Adria-
tic, an iron curtain has descended across the continent.
Behind that line lie all the capitals of the ancient states of
Central and Eastern Europe. Warsaw, Berlin, Prague, Vienna,
Budapest, Belgrade, Bucharest and Sofia, all these famous
cities and the populations around them lie in the Soviet sphere
and all are subject in one form or another, not only to Soviet
influence but to a very high and increasing measure of control
from Moscow. Athens alone, with its immortal glories, is free
to decide its future at an election under British, American and
French observation. The Russian-dominated Polish Government
has been encouraged to make enormous and wrongful inroads upon
Germany, and mass expulsions of millions of Germans on a scale
grievous and undreamed-of are now taking place. The Communist
parties, which were very small in all these Eastern States of
Europe, have been raised to pre-eminence and power far beyond
their numbers and are seeking everywhere to obtain totalitarian
control. Police governments are prevailing in nearly every
case, and so far, except in Czechoslovakia, there is no true
democracy. Turkey and Persia are both profoundly alarmed
and disturbed at the claims which are made upon them and
at the pressure being exerted by the Moscow Government. An
attempt is being made by the Russians in Berlin to build up
a quasi-Communist party in their zone of Occupied Germany
by showing special favors to groups of left-wing German
leaders. At the end of the fighting last June, the American
and British Armies withdrew Westwards, in accordance with an
earlier agreement, to a depth at some points of 150 miles
on a front of nearly 400 miles to allow the Russians to
occupy this vast expanse of territory which the Western
Democracies had conquered. If now the Soviet Government
tries, by separate action, to build up a pro-Communist Germany in their areas, this will cause new serious difficulties
in the British and American zones, and will give the defeated
Germans the power of putting themselves up to auction between
the Soviets and the Western Democracies. Whatever conclusions may be drawn from these facts - and facts they
are - this is certainly not the Liberated Europe we fought
to build up. Nor is it one which contains the essentials
of permanent peace.

(more)

**Text of Churchill's
Iron Curtain speech,
1946.** *FO 371/51624*

THIS DOCUMENT IS THE PROPERTY OF HIS BRITANNIC MAJESTY'S GOVERNMENT

SOVIET UNION.   March 28, 1946.

ARCHIVES

SECRET.   SECTION 2.

[N 4156/97/38]   Copy No.

Mr. Roberts to Mr. Bevin.—(Received 28th March.)

(No. 189.   Secret.)
Sir,
                                                   Moscow, 17th March, 1946.
        I UNDERTOOK in my despatch No. 181 to endeavour to assess the main
factors bearing upon Soviet policy, and to estimate their effect upon Anglo-Soviet
relations in the post-war world.   I am only too well aware of the magnitude of
the problem and of the difficulties of treating it thoroughly and objectively.   I
feel, however, that it must now be faced, although I submit the following review
with the greatest diffidence and in full consciousness of its inadequacies and
shortcomings.
        2.   There is one fundamental factor affecting Soviet policy dating back to
the small beginnings of the Muscovite State.   This is the constant striving for
security of a State with no natural frontiers and surrounded by enemies.   In
this all-important respect the rulers and people of Russia are united by a common
fear, deeply rooted in Russian history.   National security is, in fact, at the bottom
of Soviet, as of Imperial Russian, policy, and explains much of the high-handed
behaviour of the Kremlin and many of the suspicions genuinely held there
concerning the outside world.   Russia has always been a more backward State
than her neighbours.   Even to-day the Soviet Union, despite its prestige in the
world, is more backward than not only Britain or the United States, but than
most other European countries.   She has grown around a small principality in
Moscow, with no natural frontiers and always surrounded by unfriendly
neighbours—Tartars, Poles, Turks, Teutonic Knights and Swedes.   At the very
birth of the new Soviet State the whole world again seemed united against her,
and the fears aroused by foreign intervention after 1917 cannot yet have been
eradicated from the minds of the rulers of Russia, any more than the fear of
communism has been eradicated from that of Western leaders, who, nevertheless,
co-operated with the Soviet Union during the war.   The frontiers of Russia have
never been fixed and have gone backwards and forwards with defeats or victories
in war.   But even after her greatest victories in the past Russia has somehow
found herself deprived of many of the fruits of those victories, and has never
achieved the security which she thought her due reward.   Despite this, over the
centuries Russia has expanded, as much by peaceful colonisation (*e.g.,* in Siberia)
and by agreement with local leaders (*e.g.,* in Georgia) as by actual conquest.

Above and opposite: Foreign Office despatch from Frank Roberts to Ernest Bevin. *FO 371/56763*

~~ulated to the Cabinet by direction~~
~~the Secretary of State for Foreign Affairs~~
THIS DOCUMENT IS THE PROPERTY OF HIS BRITANNIC MAJESTY'S GOVERNMENT

14

SOVIET UNION.   March 27, 1946.

CONFIDENTIAL.   SECTION 1.

ARCHIVES

[N 4065/97/38]   Copy No. 8

Mr. Roberts to Mr. Bevin.—(Received 27th March.)

(No. 181   Confidential.)
Sir,   *Moscow, 14th March,* 1946.
    IN my despatch No. 799 of the 31st October I attempted to review Soviet
policy and the state of Anglo-Soviet relations after the breakdown of the Council
of Foreign Ministers in London. The outlook was not then entirely encouraging,
and there were clearly many danger signs ahead. But M. Molotov, making in
place of Generalissimo Stalin what is the most important annual statement of
Soviet policy, gave on the 6th November a relatively reassuring picture of Soviet
aims and in particular committed the Soviet Union to continued international
co-operation within the United Nations Organisation, and more particularly
within the framework of the Big Three. The sober hopes fostered by this statement have not, however, been borne out in succeeding months, and the time now
seems overdue to review the position once again after the visit paid by you and
Mr. Byrnes to Moscow and the meeting of the General Assembly in London, to
attempt once again to assess Soviet policy in what has been described here as the
period of peaceful reconstruction ahead, and even to consider on what basis the
Anglo-Soviet Alliance, which made so essential a contribution to the victory of
the United Nations, can do useful service in the peace.
    2. The more or less simultaneous departure from Moscow of the British,
American and French Ambassadors marks a new epoch in the relations of the
Soviet Union with the outside world. These changes have taken place at a time
when there is more anxious questioning concerning the present behaviour and
ultimate intentions of the Soviet Union than at any period since the collapse of
foreign intervention. This anxiety is by no means confined to circles normally
suspicious of the Soviet Union, and has been stated frankly and authoritatively
in your own speech on the 21st February in the House of Commons, and
subsequently by Mr. Byrnes, Mr. Vandenberg and also by Mr. Winston Churchill
in the United States. Generalissimo Stalin's reply to-day to Mr. Churchill,
following upon a growing anti-British press campaign and coupled with the
mounting tension in Persia, has brought matters to a head.
    3. When M. Molotov spoke on the 6th November a deadlock existed as
regards Soviet relations with her two major allies in the Far East and also in
the Balkans. This prevented any progress with the signing of peace treaties
even with Italy and the minor satellites. The shadow of the atom bomb darkened
our relations and behind every manifestation of Anglo-American solidarity, *e.g.*,
in Bulgaria or Roumania, the rulers of the Soviet Union, until then confident of
the overwhelming strength of the Red army, saw the menace of an Anglo-
American *bloc*, possessing this decisive weapon, and therefore capable not only of
depriving the Soviet Union of the fruits of the victories of the Red army, but
even of endangering the security which the Soviet Union had so hardly won. The
Soviet Government seemed to feel that in such an atmosphere they could make
no concessions, and, indeed, they soon began to counter-attack against Britain
as the weaker member of what they regarded as an Anglo-American combination.
Already existing difficulties in Greece, Persia and the Middle East generally, and
over the so-called "Western *bloc*" and the administration of Germany, were
intensified. A warning note was sounded for the first time since the war in
Soviet propaganda in regard to such questions as India, Egypt and colonies in
South-East Asia, issues on which the Soviet press had long been silent. Above
all, increasing attention was devoted to the renewed Marxist-Leninist ideological
campaign. Britain, as the home of capitalism, imperialism and now of social
democracy, is a main target and is shown up as the centre of opposition to the
progressive ideas and forces of which the Soviet Union claims to be the chief
patron.
    4. In this atmosphere, which clearly compromised the chances of satis-
factorily launching the United Nations Organisation, it is not surprising that the
United States Administration took fright. Mr. Byrnes, therefore, took the

[76—36]   B

ensure the active support of the United States. This was achieved in 1949, when the United States, Canada and Western European nations signed the North Atlantic Treaty providing collective security against aggression from the Soviet Union.

Western fears about communist expansion were compounded in 1949 when Mao Zedong declared himself the leader of the People's Republic of China following victory of the communist forces in the Chinese civil war. The seizure of power by the Chinese communists and subsequent alliance with the Soviet Union increased calls in the West for further military spending. In June 1950, the clamour for rearmament became unstoppable: North Korean armed forces crossed the border with South Korea and sought to unify the country under communist control. The invasion was widely seen in the West as an attempt by the Soviet Union and China to place the whole of South East Asia under communist rule. The western response to the North Korean attack was both swift and resolute. American and British forces under the authority of the United Nations mounted an immediate counter-offensive and substantially increased their defence budgets. Faced with a strong military response, the North Korean forces began to retreat. The imminent defeat of the North Koreans led China to actively intervene in support of its fellow communists. The conflict soon became deadlocked with both sides eventually agreeing to an uneasy ceasefire.

Planes being unloaded during the Berlin airlift 1948. *AIR 10/5067*

Four Douglas C-54 Skymasters on runway during the Berlin airlift, 1948. *AIR 24/1807*

Coal being loaded aboard a fleet of US C-54s during the Berlin airlift 1948. *AIR 24/1807*

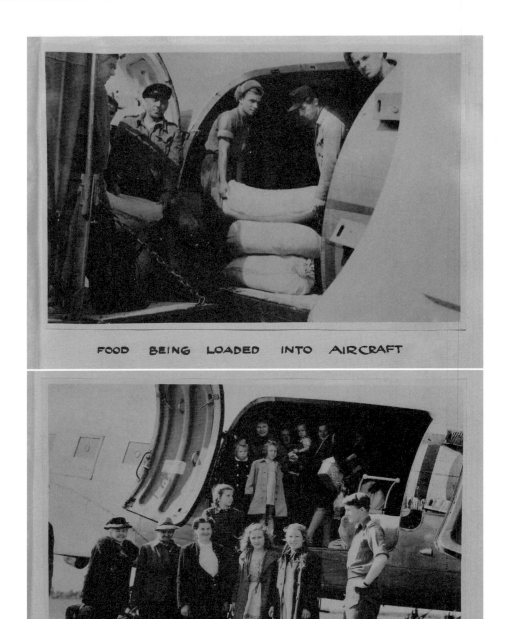

FOOD BEING LOADED INTO AIRCRAFT

PASSENGERS FROM BERLIN

Food and passengers at RAF Station Lubeck during the Berlin airlift. *AIR 55/118*

Marshall Aid cartoon. *INF 3/1295*

The impact of the Korean War on western strategy was profound. The result was NSC-68, a top secret document written by the US National Security Council that militarised the Cold War. The paper supported a significant expansion in the military budget of the United States and increased military aid to western allies. NATO agreed to increase the number of military divisions from fourteen to fifty with US forces stationed permanently in Europe. The new policy was designed to confront the Soviet Union and create conditions both economic and political to deter the Soviet Union from pursuing a military victory. To demonstrate its resolve, the US sanctioned the development of the hydrogen bomb which was vastly more destructive than the atomic bomb that destroyed Hiroshima and Nagasaki. In short, rather than coexisting with the Soviet Union, the US and its allies sought to roll back and ultimately defeat the Soviet system.

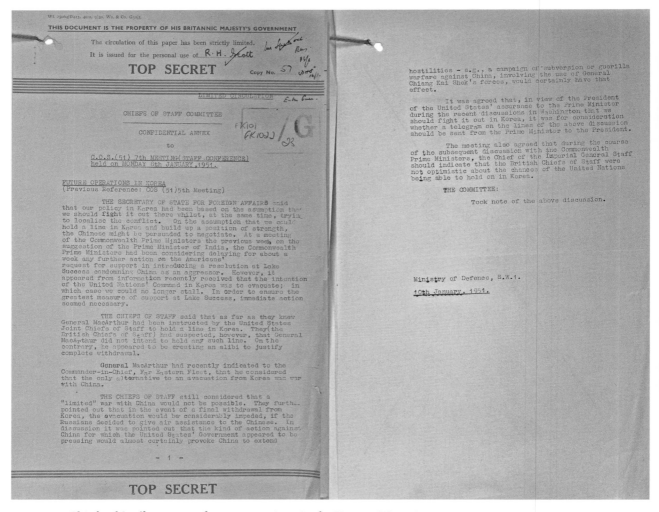

Chiefs of Staff report on future operations in the Korean War, 1951. *FO 371/92756*

In this formative period of the Cold War, the western allies relied exclusively on American air power and the use of nuclear weapons to deter Soviet aggression. Military plans covering the deployment and use of nuclear forces in defence of the West were a closely guarded American secret. Even the British, who had been a junior partner in the Manhattan Project that had designed the first nuclear bombs used against Japan, were denied access. To maintain Britain's status as a global power, the Prime Minister, Clement Attlee, authorised the development of a British nuclear weapon. In 1949, the priority given to the project was increased following the shock announcement that the Soviets had successfully detonated a nuclear device. Britain's first nuclear test was conducted in 1952 in the Monte Bello islands off the western coast of Australia. The weapon, code named Blue Danube, possessed an explosive power of fifteen kilotons and was based on the same design as the weapon detonated over Nagasaki. To credibly deploy its nuclear weapons, Britain began to develop a new generation of bombers and missiles. These plans eventually resulted in the V-Force comprising the Vulcan, Valiant and Victor long range bombers and the Blue Streak and Blue Steel nuclear armed missiles.

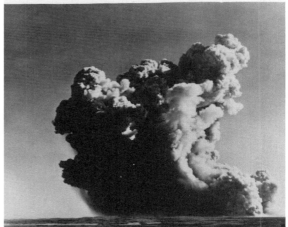

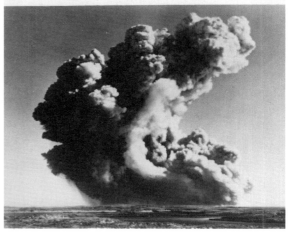

Right: **Operation Hurricane, Britain's first atomic test, October 1952.** *ADM 280/966*

Below: **British Prime Minister, Clement Attlee.** *INF 14/19*

RAF V-Force Vulcan bomber. *AIR 29/4062*

In November 1952, the former Supreme Commander of allied forces during the Second World War, Dwight D. Eisenhower, was elected President of the United States. Eisenhower, who had also served as NATO's first Supreme Commander, entered office with a promise to 'liberate' the peoples of Eastern Europe and a defence policy that emphasised the immediate and overwhelming use of nuclear weapons in response to large scale Soviet aggression. To improve its coverage of the Soviet Union, the US air force stationed nuclear capable bombers at a network of bases in both Britain and Western Europe. To strengthen America's international position, Eisenhower appointed two brothers, both supporters of a more aggressive stance against communism, to lead the State Department and the CIA. John Foster Dulles served as America's top diplomat with Allen Dulles as the nation's spymaster. Together, they helped to define American foreign policy during the 1950s.

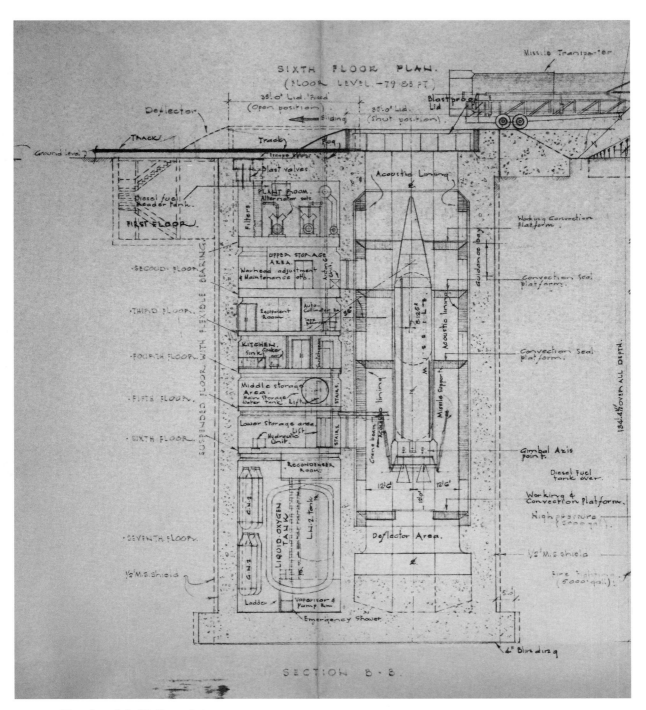

Blue Streak ballistic rocket. *DEFE 7/1392*

John Foster Dulles at Downing Street, 1953. *CO 1069/893*

The death of Soviet dictator and war time leader Joseph Stalin in March 1953 led to a relaxation of tension with the West. The new regime, under the leadership of Nikita Khrushchev, believed that confrontation with the West was no longer inevitable and sought to advance a policy of peaceful co-existence. Khrushchev led by example, attending international peace conferences and becoming the first Soviet leader to visit America in September 1959. The Soviets also supported the World Peace Council, a communist front organization that advocated universal disarmament and peaceful co-existence. The policy had major implications for the conduct of the Cold War. In the shadow of the atomic bomb, both sides realised that direct confrontation would lead to nuclear annihilation. Increasingly, the conflict between East and West became characterised as an ideological struggle between freedom and oppression with both sides mounting propaganda campaigns to win hearts and minds and secretly supporting regional insurgencies to further their aims and global ambitions.

Visit of Russian leaders to the UK, Foreign Secretary Selwyn Lloyd shakes hands with Nikita Khrushchev, 1956. *CO 1069/893*

The destructive potential of nuclear weapons and the development of more sophisticated missiles and bombers led the three nuclear powers, the United States, the Soviet Union and Great Britain, to explore ways of curbing the arms race and preventing the spread of nuclear weapons to other countries. The willingness to cooperate rather than threaten each other's systems was rewarded with some success. Two of the most far reaching agreements were the Partial Nuclear Test Ban Treaty of 1963, which prohibited test detonations in the atmosphere and under water and the Nuclear Non-Proliferation Treaty signed in 1968 which helped to halt the spread of nuclear weapons to other countries and to promote cooperation in the peaceful uses of nuclear energy.

ANNEX A

EAST-WEST RELATIONS

Introduction

Over the whole spectrum of international affairs, the Soviet leaders seem to have arrived at the belief that no important world problem can any longer be settled without their agreement. This belief is reflected in their toughness of attitude on individual problems such as Laos and disarmament; it is institutionalised in the *troika* proposal, involving a built-in veto on any executive action, which they have now put forward in relation to nuclear tests as well as to the United Nations Secretariat.

2. On Germany and Berlin the Russians go further; they seem to believe that they are now strong enough in this particular context to impose or negotiate a settlement which would involve at the very least an important consolidation of their position in Eastern Europe. The following are some of the causes of their determination to pursue a forward policy.

Soviet Strength

3. Militarily, Mr. Khrushchev has said, even the most inveterate enemies of the Soviet Union now concede that she is the strongest Power in the world. Economically, Russia expects to overtake the United States in total production by 1970 and in *per capita* production soon afterwards. Mr. Khrushchev may not entirely believe these claims, and he certainly does not want to put the first to the test of war, but they colour his whole thinking.

4. Internally, the Soviet Union is on the eve of the XXIInd Party Congress. The chief item on the agenda is expected to be the transition from socialism (characterised in Soviet thinking by the slogan " to each according to his work ", and involving strict controls) to communism (a state of comparative economic plenty—" to each according to his need "). It is possible that a definite schedule will be laid down for the progress of the Soviet Union towards communism. Against the background of severe agricultural shortcomings, and a good deal of openly acknowledged and criticised apathy and spivvery, it seems doubtful whether there will in fact be any spectacular transition in the near future. Nevertheless some new formula is likely to be produced, the effect of which will be to bring the vision of communism appreciably closer. The significance of such a step should not be underestimated. For the true believer, communism represents the final stage of mankind's achievement in the political, economic and social spheres. The prospect of its establishment in the Soviet Union will be of millenary significance for the party, and the general public will certainly be infected by their enthusiasm since it will minister to their national pride.

5. The Russians also take comfort from what appears to them as the spread of their sphere of influence abroad. As they are fond of saying, one-third of the world's population now live under socialism. And although it is 10 years since communists came to power in any country, their power and prestige has much increased their capacity to win friends and influence people (if only by frightening them).

Capitalist Weakness

6. The counterpart of the advancement of socialism is the decay of capitalism. Here again, to Russian eyes, events have only confirmed the predictions of Marx and Lenin. In " the decisive sphere of human endeavour, the sphere of material production ", the West is falling behind in rate of growth. In the Soviet Union industrial production is increasing by 10 per cent. a year, compared with 3 per cent. in the United States. In addition, the Russians see evidence of our decadence in our economic difficulties and social problems. Mr. Khrushchev's " worn-out mare of capitalism " is much more than a figure of speech for him and for his audiences. Indeed many of the latter are probably more confident of our decline than they are of their own progress. The idea of a gradual transformation of capitalism, undetermined by Marxist influence, is quite foreign to Marxist or Russian logic.

TOP SECRET

Cabinet paper discussing East-West relations, July 1961. *CAB 129/105*

226

55

TOP SECRET

ANNEX B

SOVIET MEMORANDUM ON ENDING NUCLEAR WEAPON TESTS

The Soviet Government considers it necessary to present its considerations on the question of ending atomic and hydrogen weapon tests. It is known that negotiations between representatives of the USSR, the United States and Great Britain at Geneva have been going on for more than two and a half years. However, there are still great difficulties in the road to the conclusion of an agreement.

The Soviet Union has done and is continuing to do everything it can to come to terms with the United States and Great Britain on a treaty to end nuclear weapon tests. It is known that in order to remove obstacles to agreement it has made substantial concessions to the Western partners in the talks, having accepted a number of proposals submitted by them.

The position of the Soviet Government at the Geneva talks is simple and clear. The Soviet Union wants nuclear weapon tests of all kinds to be ended everywhere and for all time. But the Soviet Government cannot agree and will never agree to the test-ban treaty becoming an empty scrap of paper which could be used as a cover for further experiments with nuclear weapons for the purpose of improving them and developing new means of mass destruction. There can be no exemptions from the treaty: all kinds of nuclear weapon tests must be banned—in the air, underwater, underground and in outer space.

In view of the present unsatisfactory position at the Geneva Conference, the Soviet Government should like to state once more its position on fundamental issues which remain unresolved to this day.

Question of a Moratorium

It is known that the Soviet Government agreed to the American proposal that the treaty should temporarily exclude from the ban underground tests of nuclear weapons below a definite threshold value. Now we must reach agreement on a moratorium on underground nuclear explosions temporarily not covered by the treaty.

It goes without saying that the agreement on a moratorium must be of such a nature that no State could violate it arbitrarily and resume test explosions of nuclear bombs. In view of this, the Soviet Government is firmly convinced that the expiration of the moratorium, an agreement on which would be reached by the parties concerned, should not absolve States of their commitment not to hold underground nuclear explosions.

Question of Control

The Soviet Union, just as the United States, considers that strict international control must be established over the cessation of the tests. However, it is quite obvious that this control can be effective only if it rests on the mutual consent of the sides and not on the desire to take advantage of the control machinery to impose the will of one group of States upon another group.

The Soviet Government has examined all aspects of the question how to safeguard equal rights of the sides in the implementation of control, and has drawn the firm conclusion that the staffing of the control agencies must be based on equal representation of the sides. It is precisely in conformity with this principle that the Soviet Union proposes that an understanding should be reached on the composition of the chief executive agency—the administrative council.

The refusal to accept the proposal on instituting an administrative council of three equal representatives, one each from the principal groups of States—the socialist States, the countries belonging to Western military *blocs,* and the neutralist States—is being justified by allegations that the Soviet Union seeks to obtain some special rights in the control organisation. This assertion, of course, has no foundation whatsoever.

TOP SECRET

59331   B

Soviet memorandum on ending nuclear tests, July 1961. *CAB 129/105*

Peaceful co-existence was not always harmonious. Both sides conducted military exercises and covert operations to test the other's resolve and willingness to support their allies. In Berlin, Khrushchev demanded the immediate expulsion of all western forces. This led to a tense standoff and the construction of the Berlin Wall which soon became a potent symbol of the East-West divide. The most dangerous nuclear crisis took place in October 1962 in the Caribbean, when the Soviets secretly installed nuclear missiles on the island of Cuba, ninety miles off the coast of Florida. The leader of Cuba was Fidel Castro, a Marxist revolutionary who sanctioned deployment of the missiles to protect Cuba from US invasion and strengthen international communism. The missile sites were soon discovered by a U-2 spy plane. To prevent further shipments and force the removal of the missiles, the US mounted a naval blockade of the island. In a nationwide televised address, President Kennedy announced that any nuclear missile launched from Cuba would be seen as an attack on the United States and result in a full retaliatory response against the Soviet Union. The crisis was eventually resolved after the Soviet leader Nikita Khrushchev agreed to remove the missiles from Cuba in exchange for a promise by the US not to invade Cuba.

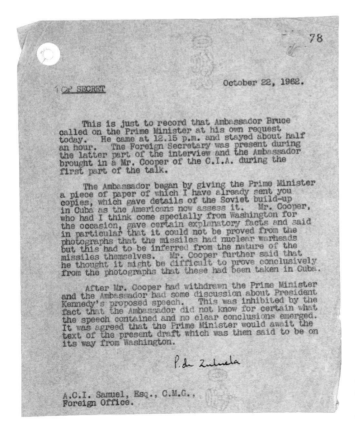

Cuban missile crisis
US Ambassador visits the
Prime Minister. *PREM11/3689*

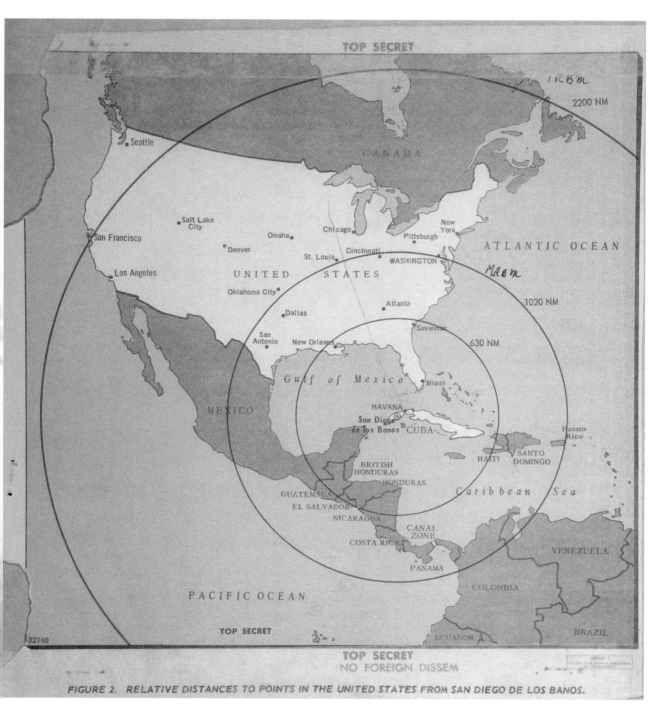

TOP SECRET

FIGURE 2.   RELATIVE DISTANCES TO POINTS IN THE UNITED STATES FROM SAN DIEGO DE LOS BANOS.

Range of missiles fired from Cuba. *PREM 11/3689*

Subject

112

TOP SECRET

FROM WASHINGTON TO FOREIGN OFFICE

PRIME MINISTER'S

Cypher/OTP

PRISEC

PERSONAL TELEGRAM

Sir D. Ormsby Gore

SERIAL No. T487/62

No. 2630   D.   7.13 p.m. October 21, 1962
October 21, 1962   R.   7.31 p.m. October 21, 1962

EMERGENCY
DEDIP
TOP SECRET

    Personal for Prime Minister from Ambassador.

    I have just come from seeing the President. He will be
sending you an extremely important message on Cuba by teletype
machine to Admiralty House at about 10 p.m. today London time.
I think it essential you should be there to receive it
immediately. The President particularly stressed that not
only are the contents of the message confidential in the
highest degree but that the fact that you are receiving a
message at this time should on no account become known.

    [Copies sent to the Prime Minister]

F F F F

TOP SECRET

Cuban missile crisis, Foreign Office telegram to the Prime Minister. *PREM 11/3689*

US Army Missile Command, 1962. *DEFE 13/323*

Advances in Soviet missile technology placed Britain's defences under renewed threat. It was estimated that a surprise Soviet missile strike from launch sites based in western Russia would provide the government with only four minutes warning of attack before the country was destroyed in a nuclear firestorm. During this short period, the Thor ballistic missile squadrons in the UK would need to be alerted and Britain's V-bomber force scrambled, launched and issued with the order to retaliate with nuclear weapons before they were destroyed on the ground. The credibility of Britain's deterrent was placed in further doubt by the deployment of Soviet air defence missiles which threatened to destroy the V-bombers before they reached their targets inside Russia. The deployment of the Blue Steel missile which was fired 100 miles outside Soviet airspace, helped to maintain the effectiveness of the airborne deterrent into the mid-1960s.

Blue Steel nuclear missile. *AIR 29/3452*

To provide an assured second-strike capability, Britain opted to deploy a seaborne deterrent. This involved the launch of nuclear missiles from submarines which could operate virtually undetected in the deep oceans. Britain's first submarine launched nuclear deterrent entered service with Royal Navy in 1968. When fully deployed, the force comprised four Resolution class submarines each fitted with sixteen nuclear tipped ballistic missiles. The submarines and nuclear warheads were constructed and developed in the UK with the Polaris missiles supplied by the United States under the terms of the Nassau Agreement signed by US President John Kennedy and the Prime Minister Harold Macmillan in December 1962. The vulnerability of fixed launch sites on land led to the withdrawal of the Thor missile squadrons and the cancellation of Blue Streak, Britain's independently developed medium range ballistic missile. The rocket was later used as the first stage of the Europa satellite launch vehicle.

In the aftermath of the Cuban missile crisis, the two superpowers agreed to install a direct hotline between Washington and Moscow allowing both countries to quickly communicate with each other in a time of urgency, and reduce the chances that future crises could

Thor missile stationed in UK. *AIR 27/2954*

escalate into all-out war. By the 1970s, in a further effort to lessen international tension and reduce the risk of accidental nuclear war, both sides agreed to a series of regular meetings designed to build confidence between the two superpowers. The process was known as détente and was marked by a number of important arms control measures. Three of the most far-reaching, which were all signed in 1972, include the Strategic Arms Limitation Treaty (SALT) that limited the number of intercontinental ballistic missiles deployed by each side; the Biological Weapons Convention which prohibited the development and stockpiling of an entire category of weapon and the Anti-Ballistic Missile Treaty that limited the deployment of these systems to two sites in each country.

The process of détente reached its high point in 1975 with the Conference on Security and Cooperation in Europe (CSCE). This resulted in the Helsinki Accords, a comprehensive series of agreements that addressed economic, political, and human rights. The CSCE also formalised the post Second World War borders in Europe which was widely seen by commentators as a major concession to the Soviet Union. In return, Moscow agreed to respect the human rights of its citizens. This agreement left the Soviets vulnerable to criticism concerning its treatment of dissidents which soon became a major cause of contention between East and West. The era of cooperation between the superpowers reached its highpoint in July 1975, with the launch of the joint US-Soviet space flight. The docking of the Apollo and Soyuz space craft followed by the exchange of gifts between the two crews became a potent symbol of détente as the space station circled the globe.

The period of détente and international cooperation was brought to an abrupt end in 1979 when Soviet armed forces invaded Afghanistan in support of the pro-Moscow regime in its fight against anti-communist guerrillas. It was a watershed event of the Cold War, marking the first and only time that the Soviet Union had invaded a country outside the Eastern Bloc. There was further concern that the Soviets would use Afghanistan as a springboard to undermine pro-western regimes in the region. The invasion was met by worldwide condemnation, with western powers imposing sanctions and providing military aid and assistance to the Afghan rebels. The US also led a boycott of the 1980 Summer Olympics held in Moscow. The forthright western response alarmed the Soviet leadership and led to an escalation and intensification of Cold War tensions.

The election of Margaret Thatcher as British Prime Minister in 1979 followed by the election of Ronald Reagan as US President in 1980 further increased international tension. Both leaders were elected on a platform of confronting Soviet aggression and strengthening the Anglo-American alliance. A major concern was the Soviet deployment of the SS-20 missile. This was a mobile system which increased the flexibility of the Soviet's nuclear arsenal. To counter the SS-20, NATO agreed to deploy cruise and Pershing missiles in Western Europe. This decision was opposed by many in the West who believed nuclear weapons were morally wrong. In Britain, a women's peace camp was established

Soviet Tu-16 Badger bomber over the North Atlantic, 1970. *AIR 28/1838*

outside Greenham Common airbase to protest against the deployment of cruise missiles at the base. The international environment became further strained in December 1981 following the imposition of martial law in Poland. The crackdown was ordered by the communist party to crush a series of popular uprisings coordinated by the independent trade union Solidarity. In September 1983, Soviets fighter planes shot down a South Korean passenger jet after it strayed into Soviet airspace over the Kamchatka peninsula, killing all 269 passengers and crew.

To counter advances in Soviet missile technology, President Reagan announced plans to deploy a space-based system to defend the US mainland from attack. The system, known as the Strategic Defense Initiative, envisaged the deployment of advanced weapons systems including lasers, particle beam accelerators and satellites designed to destroy incoming missiles in space before they reached their intended targets. Reagan was a strong supporter of SDI, believing that the doctrine of mutually assured destruction was a suicide pact and that the US mainland needed a protective shield. The concept soon became known as 'Star Wars' after the science fiction films set in space created by George Lucas. It was criticised as both expensive and destabilising and adding yet a further dimension to the arms race.

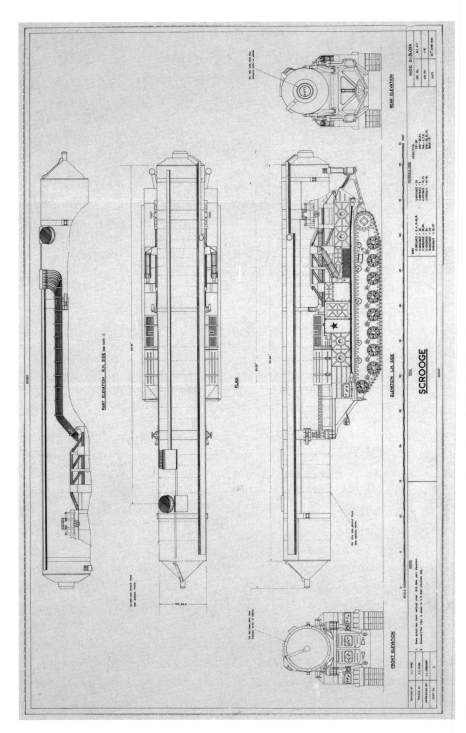

Elevations of Russian SS-15 Scrooge Intercontinental Ballistic Missile, 1965. *DEFE 44/163*

The Soviets saw SDI as a means of neutralising its strategic missile force and facilitating a nuclear first strike. The development of countermeasures placed further strains on the faltering Soviet economy.

The deployment of Pershing and cruise missiles coupled to SDI convinced the Soviet leadership that NATO was preparing to attack the Soviet Union in a surprise nuclear first strike. Soviet paranoia was not helped by the aging leadership of the regime. Following the death of the long-serving Soviet leader Leonid Brezhnev in 1982, the Soviet Union was led by a succession of old men who had little experience of the outside world. Brezhnev's successor was the 68-year-old former head of the Secret Police, Yuri Andropov, who died after one year and eighty-nine days in office. Andropov was replaced as leader by the enfeebled 72-year-old former party propagandist Konstantin Chernenko, whose time in office was even shorter, lasting one year and twenty-six days. In 1985, the leadership of the Communist Party passed to a younger generation when the comparatively sprightly 54-year-old Mikhail Gorbachev was appointed the eighth and last leader of the Soviet Union.

Gorbachev immediately began to liberalize Soviet society and reform the economy which had stagnated during the Brezhnev era. He also sought to improve relations with the United

Aircraft carrier HMS Ark Royal and the guided missile destroyer HMS Devonshire on exercise in the Mediterranean, May 1963. *DEFE 7/1717*

States and lessen the danger of nuclear war. In a series of summits at Geneva and Reykjavik, both sides agreed to work together to halt the nuclear arms race. This process culminated in the 1987 Intermediate-Range Nuclear Forces (INF) Treaty, which eliminated a whole family of nuclear-capable ground-launched ballistic missiles and cruise missiles with ranges between 500 to 5,500 kilometres. Gorbachev also rejected the 'Brezhnev Doctrine', which gave the Soviet Union the right to provide militarily support to fellow communist states if their governments were threatened by internal revolt. To demonstrate his peaceful intentions, he announced the withdrawal of 500,000 Soviet troops from Central and Eastern Europe.

Rather than allaying public disquiet, the reforms championed by Gorbachev led to increased demands for further freedoms. In Poland, increases in food prices led to a renewed wave of strikes and civil unrest. Faced with nationwide protests, the Polish government had little option but to open negotiations with Solidarity whose membership soon reached 1.5 million. A major demand of the protesters were free elections. These were held in June 1989, with anti-communist candidates winning a landslide victory. Following Poland's lead, Hungary was next to switch to a non-Communist government and immediately began to dismantle its border fence with Austria. This increasingly destabilized East Germany and Czechoslovakia as thousands of their citizens illegally crossed over to the West. In November 1989, hundreds of thousands of people demonstrated in East Berlin, demanding free elections and access to West Berlin. Unwilling to use force, the border guards opened the gates to West Berlin. Jubilant crowds soon began to tear down the Berlin Wall, long a symbol of the division of Europe. In 1991, following a failed coup by hard-line communists in Moscow, the Soviet Union collapsed into fifteen separate independent countries. The Cold War, which had remained the driving force of international relations for almost half a century, was over.

RAF Lightning alongside a Soviet Tu-95D Bear over the North Atlantic, April 1970.
AIR 28/1838

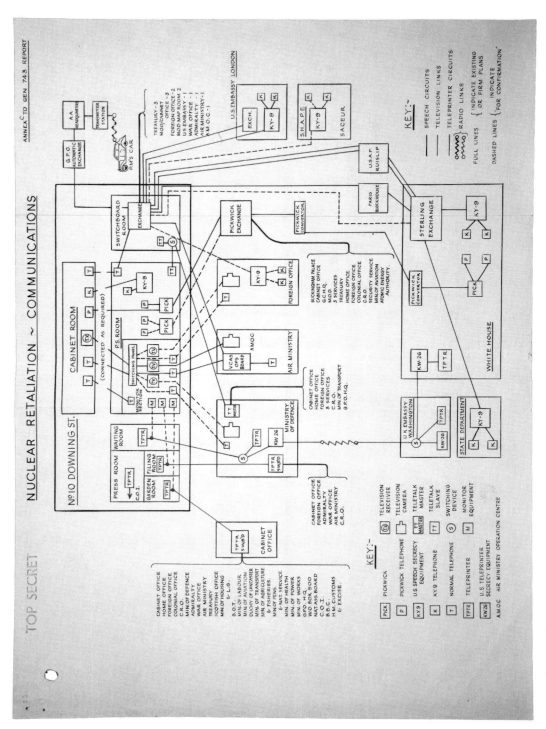

UK Nuclear retaliation procedures, 1960-1962. *DEFE 25/49*

CABINET OFFICE   0   MON 09 DEC 91 13:05   PG.03

a friduntal

POSSIBLE STATEMENT BY THE PRIME MINISTER ON THE RESIGNATION OF PRESIDENT GORBACHEV

I understand President Gorbachev's decision that, in the dramatic new situation in the Soviet Union, the time has come to pass the baton to someone else.

This week's attempted coup reminded us all of the heroic scale of President Gorbachev's achievements. He did not just respond to events. He led them. He turned the Soviet Union away from dictatorship and towards democracy. He helped the countries of Eastern Europe along the path to freedom. He replaced confrontation with the West with co-operation. He is one of the giant figures of 20th century history.

Norma and I have greatly valued our friendship with Mikhail and Raisa Gorbachev. We ~~are sure~~ will have a continuing role to play in shaping the future of ~~the Soviet Union~~ *his country* and ~~He~~ and Raisa have our warmest good wishes.

A huge responsibility now falls on the shoulders of the people of the Soviet Union and its Republics as they move to genuine democracy. We shall support them in seeking freedom with stability and responsibility.

tmw a:\foreign\gorbachev

Draft statement by the Prime Minister on the resignation of President Gorbachev. *CAB 19/3562*

CHAPTER 2

TWO TRIBES: NATO AND THE WARSAW PACT

In the immediate aftermath of the Second World War, the three victorious allies, Britain, the United States and the Soviet Union, sought to create a new world order that would guarantee peace and security. Britain and the United States initially hoped for some form of agreement with Moscow but these ambitions were soon frustrated. Stalin's determination to consolidate Soviet control over the occupied countries of Eastern Europe was seen as a direct challenge to western interests. In an impassioned speech in the House of Commons in January 1948, the British Foreign Secretary, Ernest Bevin, argued that the establishment of a defence pact between the countries of Western Europe was essential to guard against the threat posed by the Soviet Union. Bevin's intervention proved successful and resulted in the Brussels Treaty signed by the five countries of Belgium, France, Luxembourg, the Netherlands and the United Kingdom. The treaty, which came into force on 25 August March 1948, created a collective military alliance based on the shared cultural heritage of its member states.

The British believed that the countries of Western Europe, still struggling to feed and house their own citizens, were in no position to resist Soviet aggression without the help of the United States. It was hoped that the US Congress would sanction economic and military assistance to Europe before conditions deteriorated further. The Brussels Treaty was seen as a possible model which might form the basis of a transatlantic alliance. Exploratory talks to map out the details of a collective security agreement began in Washington in July 1948, with Sir Oliver Franks, the UK ambassador, representing British interests. Fundamental differences soon began to emerge. Britain's primary objective was to convince the Americans to supply arms and equipment. The United States proved unwilling to commit military resources to guarantee European security. Further disagreement centred on the size and geographical coverage of the proposed alliance, with the US wishing to include all nations bordering the Atlantic. Britain believed that a large alliance of disparate states would be unwieldly, difficult to coordinate and ineffective.

74

North Atlantic Security Pact.

(Previous Reference:
C.M. (48) 68th Conclusions, Minute 3.)

Text of Pact.

The Cabinet had before them two memoranda by the Foreign Secretary (C.P. (49) 34 and 37) on a number of outstanding points regarding the North Atlantic Security Pact.

The Foreign Secretary said that, since he circulated C.P. (49) 34, the United States Secretary of State had held informal discussions with the Senate Foreign Relations Committee, and there was every reason to believe that the committee would accept a version of Article 5 of the Pact, dealing with mutual assistance, which would be acceptable to the Brussels Treaty Powers. The latest draft made it clear, as the United Kingdom Government had always wished, that this was a matter of mutual assistance and not merely of United States support of Europe. It substituted the words " action, including the use of armed force " for the phrase " military or other action "; and another amendment recognised the right of each party to determine what action was necessary in any given circumstances. The Senate Committee wished to see a separate Article added to the Pact to the effect that the fulfilment by a signatory of obligations under the Pact should be " in accordance with established constitutional processes." The Committee were doubtful about Article 2, which dealt with cultural links, but the Canadian Government still attached importance to this Article.

In discussion the following points were made :—

(*a*) The revised version of Article 5, which the United States Secretary of State had provisionally agreed with the Foreign Relations Committee of the Senate, was satisfactory from the United Kingdom point of view and in some ways was an improvement on the original draft. It was much stronger than the draft, on which it seemed possible at one time the Senate might insist.

(*b*) The Canadian Government were anxious that the Pact should not appear to be confined entirely to military matters, and it was desirable that the United Kingdom Government should support them in their claim that Article 2 should be retained. It was recognised, however, that this Article was unlikely to have any practical effect.

(*c*) The additional Article dealing with constitutional processes might give rise to difficulties at some later date, for it might be invoked by unfriendly elements in the United States with a view to stressing the freedom of action of the parties in time of emergency. It was, however, preferable that this reference to constitutional processes should be embodied in a separate Article, rather than included as a further qualification to Article 5, and it would be expedient to accept the Article, if it were pressed, rather than run the risk of controversy in Congress.

Procedure for Signing.

The Foreign Secretary pointed out that, at present, the Brussels Treaty Powers were being consulted on Article 5; and the United Kingdom Government would not be committed to the Pact until they had seen and approved it in final form. Thereafter, the Pact might either await further negotiation and agreement with all interested countries, or it could be signed by the United States, Canada and the Brussels Treaty Powers, leaving any other States to adhere to it later. He favoured early signature by the smaller number of Powers in the first instance, since otherwise there would be long delays while negotiations were conducted with other Powers who might wish to insert in the Pact further provisions affecting their particular interests.

There was general agreement with the Foreign Secretary's views.

Mediterranean Countries.

The Foreign Secretary drew attention to the proposed declaration by the signatories of the North Atlantic Pact designed to afford some protection to Italy, Greece, Turkey and Persia. While there might be two views about this, his general impression was that the declaration would appear to weaken the obligations of this country to Turkey under the Anglo-Turkish Treaty of 1939, and President Truman's declaration of interest in Turkey and Greece.

Cabinet discussion of NATO Treaty, 1948. *CAB 128/15*

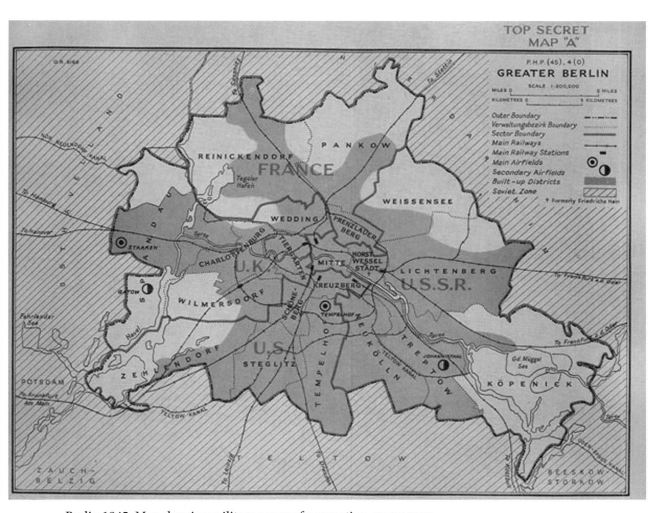

Berlin 1945, Map showing military zones of occupation. *FO 371/50831*

The wording of the treaty also proved difficult. A major sticking point was the treaty obligation covering collective defence. The Europeans favoured an agreement similar to the Brussels Treaty, under which members of the alliance agreed to give military assistance to any country that was attacked. In contrast, the Americans were reluctant to be dragged into a European war against their wishes and insisted on a looser arrangement. It was made clear that any military response by the United States would have to be authorised by the President and ratified by Congress. In September 1948, the talks were suspended due to the US Presidential election which saw President Truman returned to the White House. A major theme of Truman's election campaign was the need to contain Soviet expansion.

Ernest Bevin, MP, British Foreign Secretary.
INF 14/20

To achieve this objective, he called for the creation of a transatlantic security pact.

Truman's latest thoughts on collective defence were circulated to European governments in a draft treaty. The central issue of contention was the mechanism triggering mutual assistance. To deter Soviet aggression, the Europeans wanted a strong commitment authorising the immediate use of military force. The United States were more circumspect and insisted that any deployment of American troops should be a decision for the President alone. To satisfy both parties, Article 5 of the draft treaty was re-worded to state that an attack against one member would be considered an attack against them all. In the event of such an attack, each member would assist the party or parties so attacked. To satisfy the Americans, it was agreed that the response would be in accordance with the right of individual, or collective, self-defence as recognised under Article 51 of the United Nations Charter, including the use of armed force to maintain the security of the North Atlantic area. Bevin believed that the draft treaty met European concerns and encouraged all parties to ratify the agreement. The North Atlantic Treaty was signed by foreign ministers at a ceremony in Washington on 4 April 1949. The twelve founding members of the alliance included the United States, Britain, Canada, France, the three Benelux countries, Norway, Denmark, Iceland, Italy and Portugal. Bevin considered the creation of the NATO alliance as his greatest achievement during his time as Foreign Secretary.

To become an effective military force, NATO needed to bring together the armed forces of its twelve member states and start to develop a coordinated military strategy to counter Soviet aggression. The first steps to achieve this occurred in 1950, when General Eisenhower was appointed NATO's first Supreme Commander. In its formative years, military planning and force structure within NATO focussed on matching the Soviet predominance in ground forces. Initially, alliance members sought to match these levels. Despite Eisenhower's best endeavours, it soon became apparent that NATO governments were not prepared to fund a large scale conventional build up. In 1954, NATO approved the deployment of tactical nuclear weapons within Europe. In sanctioning deployment, alliance members sought to deter Soviet aggression without the need to match Soviet force levels. Underpinning the strategy was the belief that a Soviet conventional attack on Western Europe would be met with an overwhelming atomic assault on the Russian homelands by US nuclear forces. Known as massive retaliation, the strategy became effective NATO policy throughout the 1950s.

Military planning in NATO was hampered by uncertainty over the future role of Germany. Defeated in the Second World War, the country had been divided between East and West since 1945. In their public statements, both Washington and Moscow supported a reunified Germany but neither side was anxious to reach a settlement. In 1949, the three western powers agreed to combine their zones of occupation and established the Federal Republic of Germany. Moscow responded in kind by establishing the German Democratic Republic in East Germany. In May 1955, ten years after the defeat of Nazi Germany, the western military powers formally ended their military occupation and recognised West Germany as an independent sovereign state. Despite French reservations, West Germany sought membership of NATO and became the fifteenth member of the alliance, joining Turkey and Greece who had joined in 1952.

NATO Summit: Macmillan, Eisenhower and Secretary General Mr Spaak of Belgium, 1957.
CO 1069/893

NATO Summit Ottawa, 1958. *CO 1069/893*

Moscow expressed alarm about a rearmed West Germany and responded by establishing the Warsaw Pact, a military alliance between Soviet Russia and its Eastern European satellites including East Germany.

The admission of West Germany into NATO allowed military forces, including nuclear weapons, to be deployed closer to Soviet territory. To test its readiness, including the release of nuclear weapons, NATO forces participated in regular military exercises. One of the most far reaching took place in June 1955. Given the code name Carte Blanche, the exercise employed aircraft from Britain, America, Canada, Denmark, Greece, France and

Norway and simulated the use of tactical nuclear weapons against Warsaw Pact air bases and ground forces. The exercise lasted six days and culminated in the simulated delivery of over 300 nuclear bombs by tactical aircraft. The outcome was horrifying, with casualties estimated at 1.7 million dead and 3.5 million wounded. The exercise raised public concern over the stationing of nuclear weapons in Europe and plans for their use in a crisis. It also gave succour to activists in the peace movement who increased their demands for nuclear disarmament and an end to the arms race.

The division of Germany into East and West focused attention on the future status of Berlin. Still under military occupation and located deep inside East Germany, the divided city remained an obstacle to Soviet ambitions. In November 1958, the Soviet leader Nikita Khrushchev issued an ultimatum demanding the removal of western military forces from West Berlin within six months. In issuing the ultimatum, Khrushchev sought to stem the flow of East German citizens to West Berlin, which was estimated at 200,000 people a year. Financially, the loss of skilled workers was a costly drain on the East German economy and threatened to bring industry to a halt. In political terms, the exodus to a better life in the West was an embarrassment to Moscow, undermining its claims that East Germany was a socialist utopia. Khrushchev also criticized the western powers for turning Berlin into a nest of spies and attempting to subvert the East German state by stealth. To resolve the issue, Khrushchev demanded that the military occupation of West Berlin was brought to an immediate end and that the Soviet Union intended to sign a peace treaty with East Germany. He further warned that if the western powers refused to remove their troops, Moscow would act unilaterally, giving the East German regime full control of the access points into Berlin.

Khrushchev's ultimatum presented the West with a dilemma. The prospect of mounting a successful repeat of the 1948 airlift was no longer possible. The increase in West Berlin's population coupled to advances in Soviet air defences, meant that aircraft would be unable to land in the numbers required to feed the population. The west of the city now held hostage, the issue threatened to turn into a major East-West confrontation. Meeting in Washington to celebrate its tenth anniversary, NATO governments expressed their determination to maintain the freedom of West Berlin and warned Khrushchev that Soviet provocations would be met with a unified western response. To reduce tensions, the two sides agreed to meet at Geneva in the summer of 1959 to negotiate a new international agreement on the future status of Berlin. The talks were a partial success. Khrushchev withdrew his ultimatum for the withdrawal of western forces but reaffirmed his ambition of absorbing the whole of Berlin into East Germany.

In the summer of 1961, Khrushchev re-issued his ultimatum and once again gave the western powers six months to leave Berlin. The new US President, John F. Kennedy, responded by mobilising 150,000 reservists and ordering the Pentagon to begin preparations for a potential conflict over access to the city. The resolve of the West to defend Berlin was soon put to the test. In August 1961, the East German government ordered the construction of a barrier separating the two halves of the city and preventing movement from East to West Berlin. Initially constructed of barbed wire, the barrier soon began to take on a more permanent character with concrete walls and watchtowers stretching for twenty-seven miles across the centre of the city. To prevent East Berliners from scaling the wall and escaping to the West, a large tract of land was cleared on the East German side of the wall with troops ordered to open fire on anybody entering the prohibited zone. The western powers condemned the construction of the Berlin Wall which soon became a potent icon of the Cold War division of Europe.

The standoff in Berlin soon escalated into one of the tensest moments in the Cold War. In October 1961, an American diplomat was stopped in his car and refused entry to the eastern sector of the city. The US issued an official protest and demanded that all accredited diplomats were granted unimpeded access to the whole of the city. To emphasis the point, US tanks were visibly deployed close to the border checkpoint. These were soon joined by a battalion of Soviet tanks which were stationed on the other side of the border. NATO responded by raising its alert level and preparing its forces throughout Europe. For forty-eight hours, the two sides faced each other armed with live ammunition awaiting the order to fire. President Kennedy was acutely aware that a war in Europe would quickly escalate and suggested to Khrushchev that both sides remove their tanks and return to the negotiating table. For the remainder of the Cold War, western military units would remain in West Berlin to demonstrate Allied rights to the city.

The fear that a localised military dispute could escalate into all out nuclear war increasingly began to concern NATO members. The problem was the strategy of massive retaliation which gave no flexibility to military commanders. In effect, NATO had only two options – unconditional surrender or unleashing nuclear holocaust. The issue was eventually resolved in December 1967, when NATO agreed to replace the doctrine of massive retaliation with a new strategic concept. The strategy was known as flexible response and consisted of a menu of options involving the use of conventional forces as well as nuclear weapons. NATO also sought to stabilise and eventually reduce force levels in Europe. The result was the Conference on Security and Cooperation in Europe (CSCE) which opened in Helsinki in 1973. The final agreement, known as the Helsinki Accords, was signed in 1975 by thirty-five states and recognized the inviolability of the Second World War frontiers in Europe. It further obliged all the signatory nations to respect human rights and to cooperate in economic, scientific, humanitarian, and other areas of mutual concern. Military issues were dealt with by the Mutual and Balanced Force Reduction (MBFR) talks which took place in Vienna.

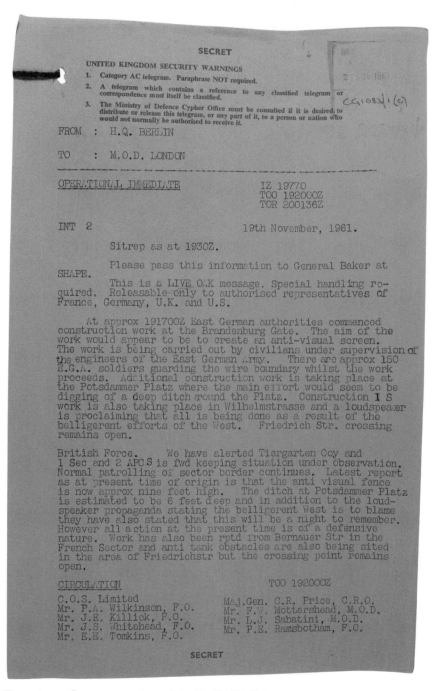

SECRET

UNITED KINGDOM SECURITY WARNINGS

1. Category AC telegram. Paraphrase NOT required.
2. A telegram which contains a reference to any classified telegram or correspondence must itself be classified.
3. The Ministry of Defence Cypher Office must be consulted if it is desired, to distribute or release this telegram, or any part of it, to a person or nation who would not normally be authorised to receive it.

CG1083/1(c)

FROM : H.Q. BERLIN

TO   : M.O.D. LONDON

OPERATIONAL IMMEDIATE   IZ 19770
                                         TOO 192000Z
                                         TOR 200136Z

INT 2   19th November, 1961.

          Sitrep as at 1930Z.

          Please pass this information to General Baker at
SHAPE.
          This is a LIVE OAK message. Special handling re-
quired. Releasable only to authorised representatives of
France, Germany, U.K. and U.S.

          At approx 191700Z East German authorities commenced
construction work at the Brandenburg Gate. The aim of the
work would appear to be to create an anti-visual screen.
The work is being carried out by civilians under supervision of
the engineers of the East German Army.   There are approx 150
E.G.A. soldiers guarding the wire boundary whilst the work
proceeds. Additional construction work is taking place at
the Potsdammer Platz where the main effort would seem to be
digging of a deep ditch around the Platz. Construction I S
work is also taking place in Wilhelmstrasse and a loudspeaker
is proclaiming that all is being done as a result of the
belligerent efforts of the West.   Friedrich Str. crossing
remains open.

          British Force.   We have alerted Tiergarten Coy and
1 Sec and 2 APCS is fwd keeping situation under observation.
Normal patrolling of sector border continues. Latest report
as at present time of origin is that the anti visual fence
is now approx nine feet high.   The ditch at Potsdammer Platz
is estimated to be 6 feet deep and in addition to the loudspeaker propaganda stating the belligerent West is to blame
they have also stated that this will be a night to remember.
However all action at the present time is of a defensive
nature. Work has also been rptd from Bernauer Str in the
French Sector and anti tank obstacles are also being sited
in the area of Friedrichstr but the crossing point remains
open.

CIRCULATION   TOO 192000Z

C.O.S. Limited
Mr. P.A. Wilkinson, F.O.   Maj.Gen. C.R. Price, C.R.O.
Mr. J.E. Killick, F.O.   Mr. F.W. Mottershead, M.O.D.
Mr. J.S. Whitehead, F.O.   Mr. L.J. Sabatini, M.O.D.
Mr. E.E. Tomkins, F.O.   Mr. P.E. Ramsbotham, F.O.

SECRET

Reports on the construction of the Berlin Wall, 1961. *FO 371/160572*

Watch tower on the Berlin Wall, 1962. *FO 371/163597*

The MBFR negotiations lasted for over fifteen years and was the only forum in which NATO and the Warsaw Pact were in direct dialogue throughout the Cold War.

The period of détente was brought to an abrupt end by the deployment of the Soviet SS-20 missile and its military invasion of Afghanistan in 1979. The SS-20 was a solid fuel intermediate-range ballistic missile with a nuclear warhead which had the capacity to destroy NATO bases and installations with little warning from launch sites deep inside Soviet territory. To counter the SS-20, NATO agreed to the deployment of 108 Pershing and 464 ground-launched cruise missiles within Europe. The decision to station cruise missiles in Britain led to the growth of the peace movement who opposed the deployment and sought to abolish all nuclear weapons. The protests centred on the RAF base at Greenham Common which was the main site for the storage of cruise missiles. In 1981, a women's peace camp was established

Above: **Access between East and West Berlin, 1962.** *FO 371/163600*

Right: **Construction of the Berlin Wall, 1962.** *FO 371/163600*

American troops in Berlin, 1962.
FO 371/163600

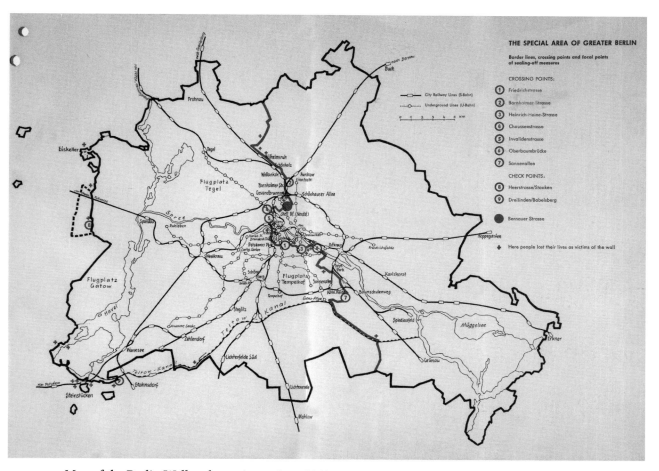

THE SPECIAL AREA OF GREATER BERLIN

Border lines, crossing points and focal points
of sealing-off measures

CROSSING POINTS:

① Friedrichstrasse
② Bornholmer Strasse
③ Heinrich-Heine-Strasse
④ Chausseestrasse
⑤ Invalidenstrasse
⑥ Oberbaumbrücke
⑦ Sonnenallee

CHECK POINTS:

⑧ Heerstrasse/Staaken
⑨ Dreilinden/Babelsberg

● Bernauer Strasse

✦ Here people lost their lives as victims of the wall

Map of the Berlin Wall and crossing points, 1962. *FO 371/163600*

in protest against the deployment of the missiles. The camp received worldwide attention and increased the profile of the anti-nuclear movement. The missiles were eventually withdrawn under the terms of the 1987 Intermediate Nuclear Forces (INF) Treaty which eliminated all nuclear and conventional ground-launched ballistic and cruise missiles with ranges between 500 to 5,500 kilometres. The INF Treaty marked the first time that both sides had agreed to remove an entire category of nuclear weapons. To enforce the treaty, both Moscow and Washington agreed to on-site inspections to verify that all missile systems had been destroyed.

In 1989, Soviet President Gorbachev announced the phased withdrawal of Soviet troops from Afghanistan and the end of the Brezhnev doctrine which sanctioned the use of force to supress popular uprisings in neighbouring socialist states. This new found freedom allowed the countries of Eastern Europe to determine their own internal affairs.

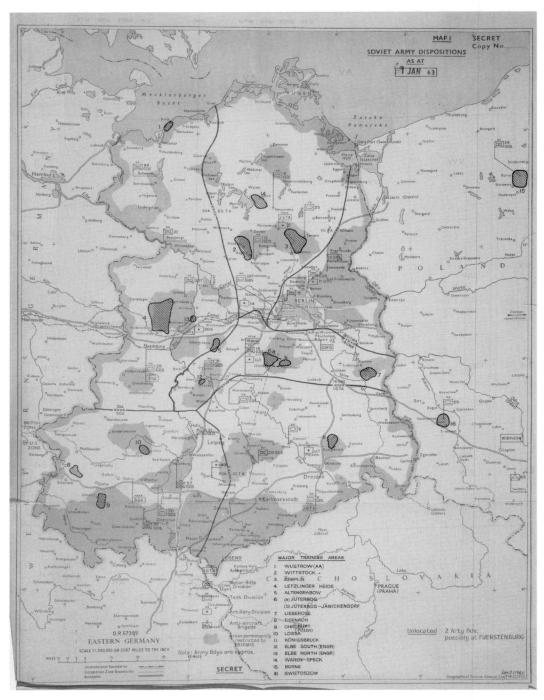

Soviet Army deployment in East Germany, January 1963. *CAB 158/48*

The result was a series of elections that brought to power reformist governments throughout Eastern Europe keen to assert national independence free from Soviet interference. The promotion of human rights and democratic freedoms articulated in the Helsinki Accords was warmly welcomed by NATO governments. The process of Soviet retrenchment culminated in November 1989 with the fall of the Berlin Wall, followed rapidly by German re-unification within the western alliance. The end of the Cold War was acknowledged by the successful conclusion of the Conventional Forces in Europe Treaty signed in November 1990 which reduced armed forces stationed in Europe to their lowest levels since 1945. In July 1991, the Warsaw Pact was dissolved, opening NATO's door to new members with the Czech Republic, Hungary and Poland joining the alliance in 1999. The future role of NATO in a post-Cold War world continues to engage governments and commentators to the present day.

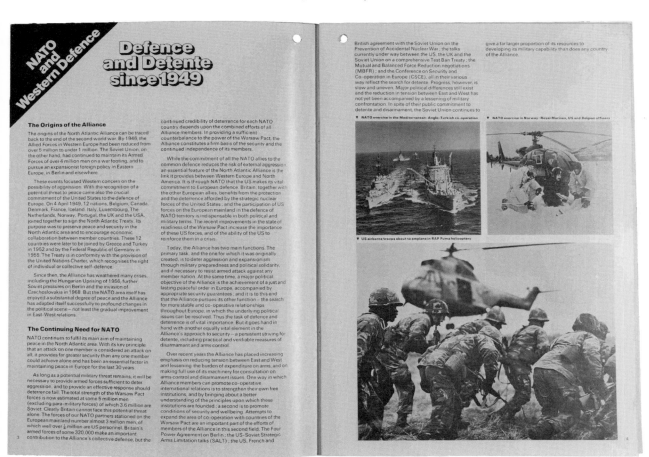

Booklet to celebrate NATO's 30th anniversary. *PREM 19/2787*

Prime Minister Margaret Thatcher laying a wreath at the wall separating East and West Berlin, 29 October 1982. *FCO 33/5871*

Keep Our Secrets Secret campaign, Telephone Talk Is Not Secure poster. *EXT 1/111*

CHAPTER 3

CARELESS WHISPER: SPIES AND TRAITORS

During the Cold War, assessing the intentions of the Soviet leadership and evaluating the capability and deployment of Warsaw Pact military forces was the primary role of western intelligence. In Britain, this function was carried out by the three intelligence agencies: the Secret Intelligence Service, commonly known as MI6, tasked mainly with covert operations overseas; the Security Service, also known as MI5, responsible for domestic counter-intelligence; and the Government Communications Headquarters (GCHQ) responsible for signals intelligence and codebreaking. The three agencies were supported in their work by the Defence Intelligence Staff housed in the Ministry of Defence with overall coordination provided by the Joint Intelligence Committee (JIC) working within the Cabinet Office. In performing its mission, British intelligence was locked in a deadly game of cat and mouse with its Soviet counterparts, the Committee for State Security, known in the West as the KGB, and the Main Intelligence Directorate of the Soviet Armed Forces, commonly referred to as the GRU.

One of the first tasks given to western intelligence during the early stages of the Cold War was to determine when the Soviets would possess a viable nuclear weapon. While nobody doubted that Moscow would develop their own bomb, estimating when this would be achieved proved difficult. The Soviet Union was a closed society and recruiting agents willing to infiltrate Soviet nuclear facilities was fraught with danger. Planning assumptions were based on the belief that, while it was possible that the Soviets would have a crude atomic device by 1951, the earliest date for the development of a fully deliverable weapon was 1954. The news of a successful Soviet nuclear explosion in August 1949 surprised the West and led to a re-examination of Soviet progress. It soon became apparent that the Soviets had managed to obtain vital secrets from the Manhattan Project. Evidence pointed to espionage and the activities of two atomic scientists, Alan Nunn May and Klaus Fuchs, who had both worked on the US bomb project during the Second World War.

2

PRIME MINISTER

SECRET INTELLIGENCE AND SECURITY SERVICES

In May, 1950, I was instructed to carry out on your behalf an enquiry into the secret intelligence and security services. No precise terms of reference were laid down; but I was asked to give special attention to three points: —

(i) The general state of efficiency of each of the secret agencies concerned with intelligence and security;

(ii) The question whether the existing allocation of resources between them is in accord with modern conditions; and

(iii) The inter-relation between them, including the distribution of Ministerial responsibility for their work.

I have completed this enquiry, and I now submit my report. Part I of the report gives a brief general description of the organisation as a whole and its total cost, and an impression of the current value of its work. Part II discusses the organisation and efficiency of the separate agencies. Part III examines their inter-relation, and the allocation of resources between them. Part IV contains some comments on the relations between the collectors and the users of intelligence. In Part V, I have made some suggestions on the co-ordination of the work of all these agencies. Part VI contains a summary of my recommendations.

In the course of this enquiry I have consulted a large number of people concerned with the subject-matter of my report, either as collectors or consumers of intelligence. I do not think it necessary to mention them by name; but I wish to express my gratitude for all the helpful advice and assistance they have given me. Mr. J. A. Drew, Ministry of Defence, and Mr. C. A. L. Cliffe, Cabinet Office, have been associated with me in the enquiry. Mr. Drew, who has long-standing contacts with the intelligence and security services, has helped me to acquire all the information which I needed; but I have not asked him to take any share of responsibility for my conclusions and recommendations. Mr. Cliffe has helped me throughout the enquiry, and I am specially grateful for his assistance in the drafting of my report.

(Signed)   NORMAN BROOK.

March, 1951.

Report on Secret Intelligence and the Security Services, 1951. *CAB 301/17*

3

Secret Intelligence and Security Services

REPORT

I

INTRODUCTION

OUTLINE OF THE ORGANISATION

1.   The three main organisations for security work and the secret collection of intelligence are:—

    (i) The Security Service (M.I.5).
    (ii) The Secret Intelligence Service (S.I.S. or M.I.6).
    (iii) Government Communications Headquarters (G.C.H.Q. or the Y Service).

M.I.5 is responsible for countering espionage, sabotage and subversive activities.   It has no executive authority, and acts through advice to Departments. Its charter, revised in 1946, speaks in terms of " the defence of the realm " and limits its sphere of action to the United Kingdom and the other countries of the Commonwealth.

The primary function of **S.I.S.** is the collection of secret intelligence by clandestine means (S.I.).   It is also responsible for the conduct of special operations (S.O.), so far as they may be authorised in peace, and for planning and preparing for the conduct of special operations work on a much larger scale in time of war. The sphere of action of S.I.S., on both the S.I. and the S.O. sides, is mainly in foreign countries.

G.C.H.Q. is the overt name for the organisation (now situated at Eastcote, but shortly to move to Cheltenham) which is responsible for breaking foreign cyphers and collecting intelligence by the interception of wireless and cable traffic.   It is also responsible for the production and security of the cyphers used by the United Kingdom Government.

2.   To complete this general outline of the intelligence organisation as a whole mention should be made here of the overt agencies, which come within the scope of this report mainly as users of secret intelligence.

The Joint Intelligence Bureau (J.I.B.), which is responsible to the Minister of Defence, provides economic, industrial and topographical intelligence which is of common interest to the three fighting Services.   It itself collects (as well as collates) intelligence from overt sources, but relies on the secret agencies for the collection of intelligence by clandestine methods.

The Intelligence Branches of the three fighting Services collate the intelligence collected and supplied to them by the secret agencies and the Joint Intelligence Bureau; but they also collect overt intelligence themselves through the Naval, Military and Air Attachés abroad, who report to their respective Directors of Intelligence.

The Directorate of Scientific Intelligence (D.S.I.), which is responsible to the Minister of Defence and is staffed by officers seconded from the Service Departments, collates scientific intelligence (other than that dealing with atomic energy) collected by the secret agencies.   It also collects and collates scientific intelligence from overt sources.

The Division of Atomic Energy in the Ministry of Supply has a particular responsibility for collating all available information on atomic research and development in all parts of the world other than the United States.   For this purpose it draws directly on the secret intelligence agencies, as well as the overt agencies, and maintains direct liaison with the atomic energy intelligence authorities in the United States.

Foreign Office posts abroad are an important source of general and political intelligence, which they collect in the course of their normal duties and pass to the Foreign Office.

40161

B 2

Report on Secret Intelligence and the Security Services, 1951. *CAB 301/17*

3

ANNEX I

RUSSIAN INTERESTS, INTENTIONS AND CAPABILITIES

1. What is Russia trying to do? How far is she capable of doing it? The present paper is intended to give the shortest answers that we can offer to these two fundamental questions.

2. We have not felt able, at this date, to assess the full implications of the recent open breach between the Cominform and the Yugoslav Government, and in particular the effect which the schism thus revealed will have on the relationship between the Soviet Government and Communist parties outside the Soviet Union. It is also too early to assess the effects of this development on Soviet policy in regard to the territories adjoining Yugoslavia, notably Austria, Trieste, Albania and Greece. Generally speaking, however, the circumstances of Tito's fall from grace bear out our view of the tight control which Russia normally expects to exert over Communist parties in other countries, and throw interesting light on the part played by the Cominform as an instrument of Russian policy.

3. It should be emphasised that in Russia's eyes the United Kingdom is still a capitalist and imperialist country, despite its Labour Government. In general the Soviet leaders are especially hostile to " reformist Socialism " of the British pattern, which they regard not only as an opponent to Communism, but also as a dangerous competitor for working-class support in many countries.

4. Our general appreciation is as follows : corresponding paragraphs in Annex II are shown in parenthesis.

Fundamental Principles

(a) The fundamental aim of the Soviet leaders is to hasten the elimination of capitalism from all parts of the world and to replace it with their own form of Communism. They envisage this process as being effected in the course of a revolutionary struggle lasting possibly for many years and assisted, should favourable conditions arise, by military action on the part of Soviet and satellite armed forces.

(b) The Soviet leaders are, however, also convinced that the capitalist world, aware of the growing strength of Communism, is likely eventually to resort to force in an attempt to avert its own collapse. This belief inspires the more immediate aim of Soviet policy, which is to ensure, by all possible means, the security of the Soviet Union. This aim is of short-term application, and is complementary to the long-term aim of establishing world Communism (paragraphs 1–10).

Capabilities

(c) It is unlikely that before 1957 the Soviet Union will be capable of supporting her armed forces entirely from the natural resources and industrial potential now under her control, in any major war, except one in which extensive operations are not prolonged. Nevertheless, if Russia wished to go to war, economic considerations would not in themselves be enough to prevent her from doing so if she felt confident of attaining her primary objectives rapidly.

(d) It is improbable that there is at present any economic objective outside the borders of the Soviet Union, or beyond her control, which she is likely to regard as essential for the fulfilment of her economic plans. The Soviet Union's economic condition appears therefore not to be, in itself, such as to impel her to use methods which might lead to a major war in order to acquire external economic resources (paragraphs 10–36).

(e) The Soviet land forces, with their close support aircraft, are sufficiently strong, at the present time, to achieve rapid and far-reaching successes against any likely combination of opposing land forces. In view of the present reduced effectiveness of the navies of the British Commonwealth, United States and the Western European Powers, the Soviet Union may appreciate that within the next few years her relative naval strength will be as great as it is ever likely to be, and that her naval situation is therefore in itself no additional deterrent against engaging in a major war. The strategic air situation, however,

35411   B 2

JIC Report: Russian Intentions and Capabilities, 1948. *CAB 158/3*

The first to be arrested was Alan Nunn May, a British physicist who had joined the Communist Party in the 1930s. During the Second World War, he worked on radar and in 1943 was transferred to Canada to assist the British team building a nuclear reactor at Chalk River near Ottawa. Once in Canada, he was approached by the Soviet Military attaché, Colonel Nikolai Zabotin and agreed to hand over classified information including two samples of uranium-235 which were flown to Moscow. At the end of the war, Nunn May returned to Britain and took up a position in the physics department at King's College, London. His espionage activities first came to light in September 1945, following the defection in Canada of the GRU cipher clerk Igor Gouzenko. The information provided by Gouzenko included over 100 documents on Soviet espionage operations. These identified Nunn May as the Soviet agent 'Alek' who had supplied Zabotin with 'useful and valuable information', including details of America's first atomic test explosion in New Mexico in July 1945. In March 1946, Nunn May was arrested in London and questioned by the Security Service. He initially denied involvement, but later pleaded guilty to breaking the Official Secrets Act and was sentenced to ten years imprisonment at Wakefield Prison in Yorkshire. Nunn May later confessed that he had pleaded guilty in order to conceal how long he had been a Soviet spy and the extent of the Russian espionage network in Britain.

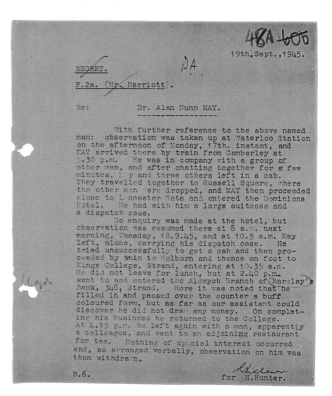

MI5 Report on Alan Nunn May.
KV 2/2209

Copy no 3.

PF. 66942 - Y.6408

Alan Nunn MAY

1. Personal Particulars.

Born: 2.5.11 at Kings Norton, Worcs. (Unmarried)

Parents: Walter Frederick Nunn MAY (Father)
Mary Annie MAY, nee KENDALL (Mother)

Identity Documents: NRIC no: A.S.A.J.379/3.
Passport No: 17701 issued at London on 27.11.42
(valid for B.E. and U.S.A.)
Formerly held Passport No: 380972 issued London 15.6.31

Photograph:

Brothers & Sister: 1. Edward W. Nunn MAY. Aged about 45 years. Married
with two children. Address: The Pump House, Barnt
Green, Worcs. A Director of Thomas Minto & Merry,
Paint Manufacturers of Birmingham.

PF. 779,869 2. Ralph Nunn MAY. Aged about 35. Married.
Address: Town House Lane, Denham, Bucks. Formerly
(1929 until at least 1937) Secretary of the National
Union of Students, 3 Endsleigh Street, WC.1; then
employed at the M.O.I.. Now apparently contemplating
going into the film business.
3. Mary. Aged about 37. Unmarried. Address: Lives
with her parents at:- Bedruthan, Barnt Green, Worcs.

MI5 Report on Alan Nunn May. *KV 2/2209*

TOP SECRET.

Telegram to NEW YORK.

No. 451.

20.2.46.

A.   [PRIMROSE] broke today as result of second M.I.5 interrogation.

B.   Herewith copy of his signed statement obtained without repeat without caution.

C.   Statement begins: "About a year ago whilst in Canada I was contacted by an individual whose identity I decline to divulge. He called on me at my private apartment in Swail Avenue, Montreal. He apparently knew I was employed by the Montreal laboratory and he sought information from me concerning atomic research.

D.   I gave and had given my careful consideration to the correctness of making sure that the development of atomic energy was not confined to the U.S.A. I took the very painful decision that it was necessary to convey general information on atomic energy and to make sure it was taken seriously. For this reason I decided to entertain the proposition made to me by the individual who called on me.

E.   After this preliminary meeting I met the individual on several subsequent occasions whilst in Canada. He made specific requests for information which were just nonsense to me - I mean by this that they were difficult for me to comprehend. But he did request samples of uranium from me and information generally on atomic energy.

F.   At one meeting I gave the man microscopic amounts of U.233 and U.235 (one of each). The U.235 was a slightly enriched sample and was in a small glass tube and consisted of about a milligramme of

Confession of Alan Nunn May. *KV 2/2212*

-2-

oxide. The U.233 was about a tenth of a milligramme and was a very thin deposit on a platinum foil and was wrapped in a piece of paper.

G. I also gave the man a written report on atomic research as known to me. This information was mostly of a character which has since been published or is about to be published.

H. The man also asked me for information about the U.S. electronically controlled A.A. shells. I knew very little about this and so could give him only very little information.

I. He also asked me for introductions to people employed in the laboratory including a man named VEALE but I advised him against contacting him.

J. The man gave me some dollars (I forget how many) in a bottle of whisky and I accepted this against my will.

K. Before I left Canada it was arranged that on my return to London I was to keep an appointment with somebody I did not know. I was given precise details as to making contact but I forget them now. I did not keep the appointment because I had decided that this clandestine procedure was no longer appropriate in view of the official release of information and the possibility of satisfactory international control of atomic energy.

L. The whole affair was extremely painful to me and I only embarked on it because I felt this was a contribution to the safety of mankind. I certainly did not do so for gain.

M. This statement has been read over by me and is the truth."

Confession of Alan Nunn May. *KV 2/2212*

Nunn May's confession was the first public proof that the Soviet Union had spied on its wartime allies and confirmed suspicions that Moscow was obtaining details of atomic research conducted in the West through its network of spies. These suspicions were later confirmed by the arrest and subsequent conviction in 1950 of Klaus Fuchs, who confessed to having spied for the Soviets during his time working on the US and British nuclear weapons projects. Fuchs was a German citizen and a committed communist who had fled to Britain following the Nazi Party's seizure of power in 1933. Fuchs initially worked as a research assistant at the University of Bristol, acquiring a PhD in physics in 1937, before taking up a scholarship at the University of Edinburgh, where he acquired a Doctorate in Science. His reputation as a brilliant nuclear physicist was cemented during this period.

Fuchs applied to be a British citizen in the summer of 1939, but following the declaration of war with Germany was interned as an enemy alien. He was eventually released and returned to Edinburgh in early 1941, where his scientific expertise led to him being recruited to join the Tube Alloys Directorate. This was the code name for Britain's nuclear weapons programme, the equivalent of the US Manhattan Project. In late 1941, following the German invasion of the Soviet Union, Fuchs contacted Russian military intelligence and offered to hand over details of British atomic research. In late 1943, Fuchs was sent to the United States to work on the Manhattan Project. Fuchs was based in New York and later at Los Alamos, the top secret atomic research facility in New Mexico. During this time, he handed over copies of many crucial research papers to Soviet intelligence. Some experts believe that the information supplied by Fuchs enabled the Soviet Union to develop and test the atomic bomb one to two years earlier than they otherwise would have done, though this is disputed.

In June 1946, Fuchs returned to England to head the Theoretical Physics Division at the UK Atomic Energy Research Establishment at Harwell. Following the arrest of Nunn May in March 1946, MI5 believed that Fuchs might also be a spy. A limited investigation was carried out but nothing of substance was discovered. Fuchs was eventually unmasked by a breach in Soviet security. The breakthrough came from US codebreakers working on a top secret project called Venona, who had managed to decipher and read thousands of Soviet telegrams sent from Washington to Moscow during the

Photograph of Klaus Fuchs, atom spy, 1951-1952. *KV 2/1245*

Second World War. Some of these messages contained reports of meetings between an agent codenamed 'Charles' who was passing atomic secrets to his Soviet handler. Further investigations were able to narrow down the list of suspects to two individuals – Fuchs and a fellow German-born scientist, Rudolf Peierls. Fuchs was brought in for questioning and interrogated several times by former Special Branch officer William Skardon. He initially denied the charges, but eventually confessed. In March 1950, he was convicted of four counts of breaking the Official Secrets Act by communicating information to a 'potential enemy' and given the maximum sentence of fourteen years in prison. Fuchs was released early due to good behaviour on 23 June 1959, and immediately departed for East Germany where he was given citizenship. He died in East Berlin in January 1988 aged 76.

The arrest and confession of Fuchs made international headlines and led to the widespread belief that the Soviets had a network of spies working undetected within the West. In America, the 'red scare' led to a series of investigations conducted by Senator McCarthy into alleged subversive activities undertaken by private individuals, public employees and organizations suspected of having Communist links. Britain was spared the worst excesses of the anti-communist witch hunts, but behind the scenes, the government acted quickly. MI5 was authorised to begin systematically vetting civil servants working in sensitive positions with a system of positive vetting introduced for all new recruits. Despite the introduction of these improved security measures, more revelations were soon to follow. In 1951, the British government was shocked to discover that two senior Foreign Office officials, Donald Maclean and Guy Burgess, were long standing Soviet agents.

The evidence against Maclean was once again supplied by Venona. A decrypted telegram revealed that an unidentified Soviet agent codenamed 'Homer' had been based in the British embassy in Washington. Further investigation narrowed the list of potential suspects down to a handful of individuals. The final breakthrough came in April 1951. A decoded message revealed that during 1944, 'Homer' had contacted his Soviet controller in New York after travelling from Washington to visit his pregnant wife. The profile matched only one person, Donald Maclean, who had recently returned to London from a posting in Cairo. Maclean had joined the Foreign Office in 1935 after graduating with a first in modern languages at Cambridge University. He quickly rose through the ranks and in 1944 was posted to Washington, where he was put in charge of atomic energy matters and was Moscow's main source on Anglo-American nuclear policy. In the 1930s, during his time at Cambridge, Maclean had been involved in communist politics and had agreed to become an agent for Soviet intelligence.

Maclean was placed under immediate surveillance by MI5. Before he could be questioned, he was visited by his colleague Guy Burgess in what appeared to be a routine social engagement. Nothing could be further from the truth. In reality, Burgess was a fellow Soviet agent who had hurriedly returned home to London from the Washington embassy to warn Maclean that he was about to be unmasked. Burgess had also been recruited by

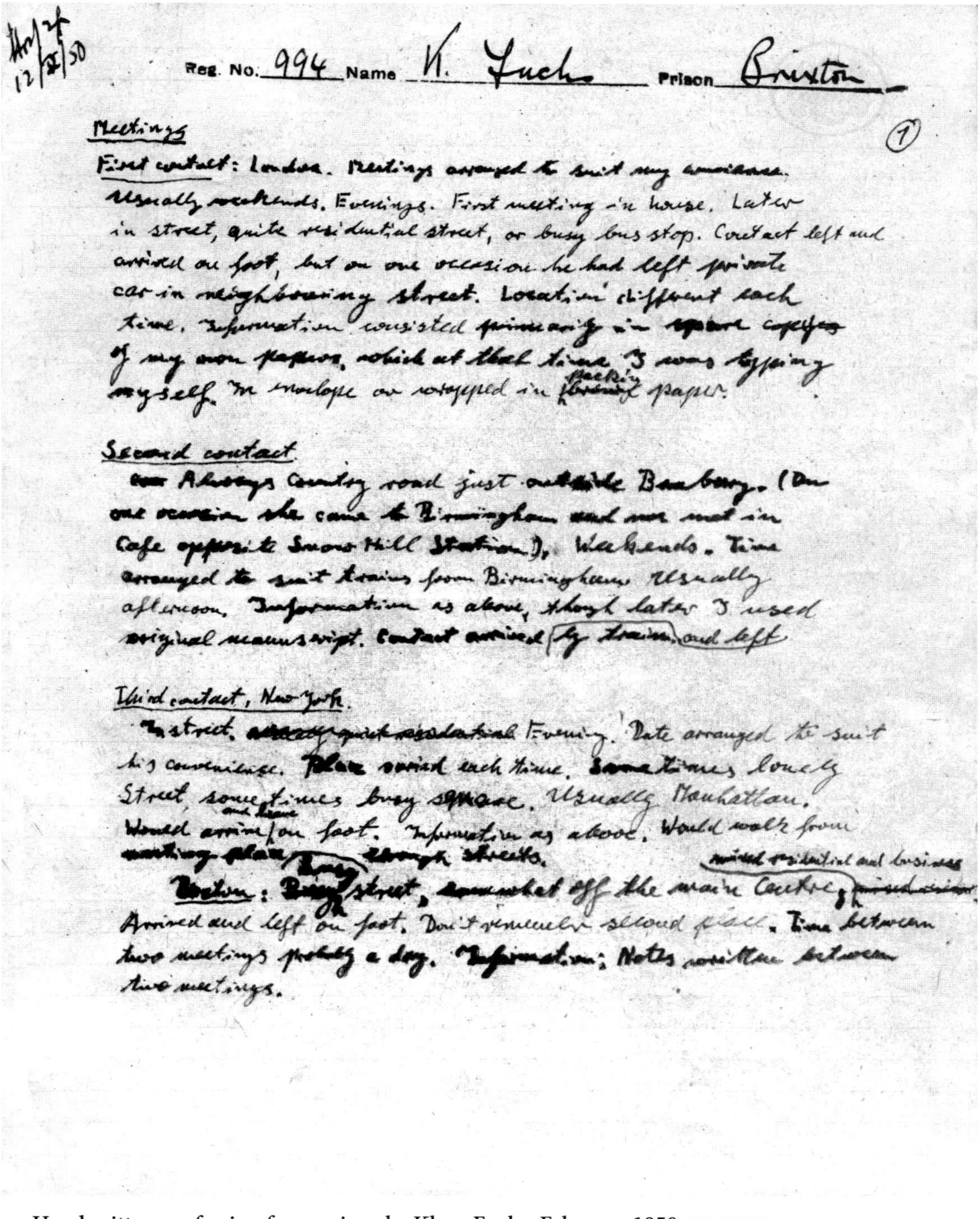

12/2/50

Reg. No. 994   Name   K. Fuchs   Prison   Brixton

(1)

Meetings

First contact: London. Meetings arranged to suit my convenience. Usually weekends. Evenings. First meeting in house. Later in street, quite residential street, or busy bus stop. Contact left and arrived on foot, but on one occasion he had left private car in neighbouring street. Location different each time. Information consisted primarily in square copies of my own papers, which at that time I was typing myself. In envelope or wrapped in packing paper.

Second contact

Always country road just outside Banbury. (On one occasion she came to Birmingham and we met in cafe opposite Snow Hill Station). Weekends. Time arranged to suit trains from Birmingham. Usually afternoon. Information as above, though later I used original manuscript. Contact arrived by train and left.

Third contact, New York.

In street. Evening. Date arranged to suit his convenience. Place varied each time. Sometimes lonely street, sometimes busy square. Usually Manhattan. Would arrive and leave on foot. Information as above. Would walk from meeting place through streets. mixed residential and business

Boston: Busy street, somewhat off the main centre. Arrived and left on foot. Don't remember second place. Time between two meetings probably a day. Information: Notes written between two meetings.

Handwritten confession from prison by Klaus Fuchs, February 1950. *KV 2/1252*

the Soviets while at Cambridge University and had subsequently worked for the BBC and MI6 before joining the Foreign Office. Burgess informed Maclean that he would soon be arrested and that they should both defect to the Soviet Union before they were caught. On the evening of 25 May 1951, both men drove to Southampton docks and boarded the night ferry to France never to return.

The disappearance of Burgess and Maclean and the subsequent investigation strongly suggested the involvement of a 'third man', who had told Burgess to return to London to warn Maclean. Suspicion immediately fell upon Harold 'Kim' Philby, who shared a house in Washington with Burgess and who had been a student at Cambridge in the 1930s. More alarmingly for London, Philby was head of the MI6 station in Washington and one of the few people with access to Venona. To uncover whether he was the third member of the Burgess and Maclean spy ring, Philby was recalled to London and interrogated by MI5. No hard evidence was found to prove his guilt. He was nevertheless tarnished by the episode and forced to resign from MI6. In 1954, Philby was named in Parliament as a Soviet agent by the Labour MP Marcus Lipton. Philby immediately denied the allegations. He was supported by the British Foreign Secretary Harold Macmillan, who contended that there was no solid evidence to support the claims. Despite his denial, many remained suspicious of Philby's loyalty. In 1961, the Soviet defector Anatoliy Golitsyn provided fresh evidence of Philby's guilt. Confronted with new information, Philby defected to the Soviet Union in 1963.

Photographs of Burgess and Maclean. *FCO 158/6*

Q 22/14(A) Q

FROM WASHINGTON TO FOREIGN OFFICE

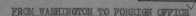

En Clair

FOREIGN OFFICE AND
WHITEHALL DISTRIBUTION

Sir R. Makins
No. 2564
October 23, 1955

D. 7.36 p.m. October 23, 1955
R. 8.35 p.m. October 23, 1955

PRIORITY

My immediately preceding telegram.

Following is text.

Begins.

London October 22.

The Mysterious "third man" whose secret warning enabled Soviet spies, Donald Maclean and Guy Burgess, to escape a counter-intelligence net and flee behind the iron curtain, will be named in Parliament after it meets Tuesday.

Norman Dodds, a Labour member today demanded that Foreign Minister Harold Macmillan unmask the tipster.   "If necessary", Dodds declared, "I will stand up in the House of Commons and name him".

Identity of this mysterious "Mr. X" has thus far been hidden by the Foreign Office.

The New York News was informed today, however, that the man Dodds will denounce is Harold A. R. Philby 38.

Philby was made First Secretary of the British Embassy in Washington in October 1949 when he was only 32, and had been in the British Foreign Service a mere two years. His rapid rise to such an important post is best explained by his real job.

Philby was in fact an intelligence agent working for the hush-hush MI-6, a branch of the British Secret Service. His Embassy assignment was only a cover for his spying activities.

Although the Foreign Office is dead sure Philby triggered the May 25 1951 flight of Burgess and Maclean, his only punishment was being fired. One reason he was sacked without fanfare is that detectives believe he was the Russian spies' unwitting dupe, that he did not even know they were traitors.

/In a ....

Kim Philby named of the 'Third Man' in Parliament. *FCO 158/175*

The defection of three senior officials who had been recruited by Soviet intelligence at Cambridge University in the 1930s led to a series of investigations to uncover other potential members of the Cambridge spy ring. The fourth member to be exposed was Sir Anthony Blunt, who had worked for MI5 during the war. He later became director of the Courtauld Institute and Surveyor of the Queen's Pictures, receiving a knighthood in 1956. In 1964, Blunt was confronted with evidence that he had spied for the Soviets during the war. In return for a full confession, the government agreed to keep his spying career a secret and granted him full immunity from prosecution. In 1979, Margaret Thatcher named Blunt as the 'fourth man'. Retribution was swift. He was forced to resign from his public positions and stripped of his knighthood. Unlike his fellow spies he remained in London and died of a heart attack in 1983, aged 75. The identity of the 'fifth man' remained a public mystery until 1990, when his name was revealed by the Soviet defector Oleg Gordievsky. He was identified as John Cairncross, a Scottish-born civil servant who had worked at Bletchley Park during the war. It later transpired that he had confessed to being a spy in 1951, following the discovery of a note written by him found at Guy Burgess's London flat. He was never prosecuted. In later life, Cairncross lived in America and France, returning to Britain in 1995. He died a few months later after suffering a stroke, at the age of 82.

The Cambridge spy ring was not the only network run by Soviet intelligence during the late 1950s. An equally successful operation was the Portland spy ring, which provided Moscow with top secret

SECRET

A02446

MR SANDERS

With your letters of 10 and 11 June, you enclosed letters to the Prime Minister from Mr Ted Leadbitter MP, Mr Willie Hamilton MP and Mr Bruce George MP. All three letters asked the Prime Minister if she would comment or make a statement on allegations that the Government knows of other spies who were involved with Burgess, Maclean, Philby and Blunt, some of whom were allowed to continue working in Whitehall after their discovery and who went on to occupy positions of influence and importance. You asked for draft replies to all three.

2. These three letters are a result of the publication of the paperback edition of Andrew Boyle's book, The Climate of Treason, and of press accounts of statements allegedly made by Boyle after the book's appearance. The paperback edition of the book added very little to the original hardback version, beyond the definite indentification of "Maurice" with Anthony Blunt. In his statements to the press, Boyle seems to have talked about "another 25 moles", and to have alleged that at least three titled men, one of whom is hereditary peer and all of whom have since achieved prominent positions in public life, were investigated as possible spies following the defection of Burgess and Maclean in 1951, but that no action was taken against them because of a lack of evidence.

3. One can only speculate about the people to whom Boyle (and the three MPs who have written to the Prime Minister) is referring. The hereditary peer is widely believed - not least by himself - to be Lord Rothschild; another possible candidate is Lord Talbot de Malahide. The other people referred to could be Lord Llewelyn-Davies, Sir Michael Stewart, Sir Frederick Warner MEP, or Sir Dennis Proctor. All of them had links either through friendship or work with Burgess, Maclean or Blunt. All of them have been thoroughly investigated. Some, like Lord Rothschild have been investigated more than once and entirely cleared. Others may have been unconscious sources for Burgess, but no evidence has been found to show that they were agents of the Russian Intelligence Service.

1

SECRET

Report on Anthony Blunt. *PREM 19/3942*

details of the Royal Navy's ships and submarines. The two key members of the ring were Harry Houghton, an Admiralty clerk, and Gordon Lonsdale, a Soviet agent working under deep cover, whose real name was Konon Molody. Houghton joined the civil service in 1951 and was posted to Warsaw, where he served on the staff of the naval attaché of the British embassy. During his time in Poland, Houghton became involved in black market trading and caught the attention of the secret police. He was approached by Polish intelligence and agreed to become an agent in exchange for cash. On his return to Britain, Houghton was posted to the Underwater Detection Establishment at Portland where he began to pass classified information to his handler, Gordon Lonsdale. To gain access to top secret files, he began an affair with Ethel 'Bunty' Gee, a clerk in the records department.

Houghton persuaded Gee to pass him documents on the unlikely pretext that he was working for the Americans. He later photographed the documents and returned them to Gee. Houghton soon came under suspicion and was put under surveillance by MI5. In July 1960, a surveillance team followed Houghton and Gee to London where they met with Lonsdale in a café outside Waterloo station and handed over an envelope concealed inside a newspaper. After the meeting, Lonsdale was followed and seen visiting a bungalow in Ruislip in West London belonging to an antiquarian bookseller and his wife, Peter and Helen Kroger.

MI5 Report on Harry Houghton.
KV 2/4380

SECRET

Note. Whether it only investigation of submit this sent me now attached same sent. LH.

15a

EXTRACT

S Form 81° 5m 1.63

Extract for File No.: P.F. 795,136.   Name: HOUGHTON.

Original in File No.: S.F. 726/2.   Vol.: 2.   Serial: 55a.   Receipt Date: 28.4.60.

Original from :   Under Ref. :   Dated : 27.4.60.

Extracted on : 1.5.63.   by : JMP.   Section : R.5.
(late Defector.)

Extract from letter from   r LAVINIA   Ment: HOUGHTON.

1.   We have recently received from C.I.A. information from LAVINIA which may have a bearing on the leakage from an Attache's office in Warsaw.

2.   LAVINIA reported as follows:-

"In about 1951 an employee of the British Naval Attache's office in Warsaw was recruited. The employee had access to the secret activities and documents of the Attache. The recruitment was carried out by a Major DIATLOWICKI who died in 1959. DIATLOWICKI spoke English and had at one time studied at OXFORD.
The Name of the employee was given provisionally by LAVINIA as HUPPKENER or HAPPKENER or HUPPENKORT or some such.
The employee was transferred back to England about the beginning of 1953 and assigned to the Admiralty. Because of his importance, he was then taken over by the KGB and continued to work successfully for the KGB in London.
The WSW was interested in the source as a possible means of testing a counter-espionage operation concerned with naval affairs which the WSW was running against the British."

3.   In Sypport of the above statements, which appeared in a letter, LAVINIA provided two documents, which are attached as follows:-

Appendix "A" : Text of a letter dated 25th May 1959 from MOCZAR, Vice-Minister of the Interior, to KOKOSZYN, Chief of the WSW.

Appendix "B" : A list of 99 documents provided by the source in the period from January 1952 to November 1952.

....

WARNING
REFER TO APPROPRIATE OFFICER BEFORE USING

THIS IS A COPY ORIGINAL DOCUMENT RETAINED IN DEPARTMENT UNDER SECTION 3(4) OF THE PUBLIC RECORDS ACT 1958 NOVEMBER 2016

SECRET

On 7 January 1961, Houghton, Gee, Lonsdale and the Krogers were arrested. The Kroger's bungalow was searched and found to contain photographic material, code pads and a long-range radio transmitter. All five were charged with espionage and convicted. Houghton and Gee were sentenced to fifteen years in prison with Lonsdale given a twenty-five year sentence. The Krogers, who in reality were Soviet agents Morris and Lona Cohen, were sentenced to twenty years but later exchanged for the British citizen Gerald Brooke, who had been arrested and jailed by the Russian authorities for smuggling anti-Soviet leaflets.

The ability to recruit and successfully run agents over a long period of time was not the sole preserve of the Soviet Union. In the early 1960s, British intelligence recruited Oleg Penkovsky, a senior officer in Soviet military intelligence. Initial contact was made via

Photograph of Houghton's house. *KV 2/4385*

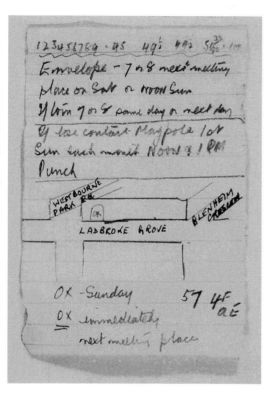

Above: Note found in Houghton's possession detailing instructions to contact his Soviet handler. *KV 2/4385*

Right: MI5 report on Gordon Lonsdale aka Konon Molody. *CAB 301/403*

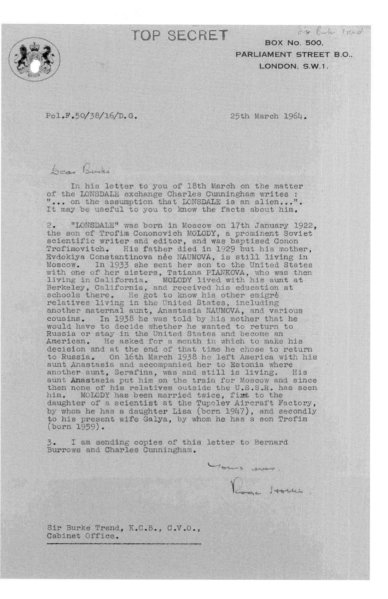

Greville Wynne a British businessman visiting Moscow who had contacts with MI6. At his first meeting, Penkovsky handed Wynne a package of confidential documents. Unsure if he was genuine or a Soviet double agent, British intelligence kept their distance. In April 1961, Penkovsky visited Britain as part of a Soviet trade delegation and was contacted by British intelligence. He agreed to a meeting and was cross examined on his background and his reasons for defecting. In exchange for money and eventual asylum in the West, Penkovsky agreed to become a defector in place maintaining his normal duties while spying for the

British. He was provided with a miniature camera and, over the next eighteen months, handed over 5,000 photographs and documents to his MI6 and CIA handlers.

The intelligence provided by Penkovsky revealed that Moscow did not possess the number of ballistic missiles claimed by the Soviet leader Nikita Khrushchev. This intelligence proved invaluable during the Cuban missile crisis of 1962, enabling the CIA to identify the missiles before they became operational. Photographic evidence of the deployment was presented to the United Nations which proved instrumental in forcing the Soviets to dismantle the sites and withdraw the missiles. On 20 October, Russian intelligence officers raided Penkovsky's apartment and discovered the miniature camera that he had used to photograph secret documents. Penkovsky was immediately arrested, found guilty of espionage and executed. During his interrogation, he revealed the name of Greville Wynne as his British contact. A few days later, Wynne was arrested at a trade fair in Budapest, Hungary, and sentenced to eight years in prison. In 1964, he was exchanged for the Soviet agent and mastermind of the Portland Spy Ring, Gordon Lonsdale.

TOP SECRET

PRIME MINISTER

The Foreign Secretary has raised with you the possibility of negotiating an exchange of Gordon Lonsdale with Greville Wynne.

Lonsdale was convicted in this country of offences under the Official Secrets Acts on 22nd March 1961, and sentenced to twenty-five years' imprisonment. Wynne was arrested in Russia on 2nd November 1962, convicted of spying on 10th May 1963, and sentenced to eight years' imprisonment.

The suggestion of an exchange raises very difficult questions which are discussed in the minute of 13th December 1963 of which I attach a copy. You may feel that it would be right for the Foreign Secretary and me to meet you in order to consider what, if anything, can be done.

I am sending a copy of this minute to the Foreign Secretary.

(SGD) HENRY BROOKE.
23rd December, 1963.

The removal of the missiles from Cuba weakened Khrushchev's position and he was replaced as Soviet leader by Leonid Brezhnev. In 1968, to consolidate his position, Brezhnev ordered Warsaw Pact forces to invade Czechoslovakia and remove the liberal reformist regime of Alexander Dubček. The suppression of the Prague Spring troubled many members of the communist party who became disillusioned with Moscow's hardline. One of these individuals was Oleg Gordievsky, a Soviet intelligence officer stationed in Copenhagen who offered his services to MI6. Gordievsky rose through the ranks and in 1982,

Letter to the Prime Minister suggesting a possible exchange of Gordon Lonsdale with Greville Wynne. *CAB 301/403*

TOP SECRET & PERSONAL

April 14, 1964.

      The Prime Minister has now given his agreement to the recommendations in Burke Trend's minute to him of April 10 about the Wynne-Lonsdale exchange, and I have been asked to put it on record to you that you should now initiate whatever action is necessary with regard to the exchange, consulting the Security Service as may be necessary. The Foreign Office will meanwhile draft and despatch through your channels a telegram to H.M. Ambassador in Moscow giving him instructions for his next approach to the Soviet authorities.

      I am sending copies of this letter to Trend, Cunningham and Hollis.

B.A.B. Burrows.

"C"

TOP SECRET & PERSONAL

Letter to the Chief of MI6 approving the Wynne-Lonsdale exchange. *CAB 301/403*

```
                       CONFIDENTIAL                        TOP COPY
              FROM MOSCOW TO FOREIGN OFFICE

Cypher/OTP                              DEPARTMENTAL DISTRIBUTION

Sir G. Harrison                            1 6 NOV 1965

No. 2408                                D.1350 15 November 1965
15 November 1965                        R.1416 15 November 1965

PRIORITY
CONFIDENTIAL

      Penkovsky Papers.

      Following for Head of Northern Department.

      We have been told in confidence by the B.B.C. correspondent
 here that Andrew Wiseman, when in Moscow recently to arrange the
 B.B.C.'s filming of Novosibirsk, was invited to lunch at short
 notice and with some urgency by Boris Belitsky (the Moscow radio
 commentator responsible for the recent Soviet commentaries on
 the "Great Train Robbery").  Belitsky's object seems to have been
 to deliver a veiled warning that any use of the "Penkovsky
 Papers" by the B.B.C.'s Overseas (and particularly Russian)
 Services could have undesirable consequences for the B.B.C.
 Belitsky also mentioned in passing that the Soviet authorities
 still had up their sleeves plenty of material embarrassing to
 Britain, including "George Blake's diary".

 2.   De Maurvy has already conveyed the substance of the above,
 less the last sentence, to the B.B.C. in London.

 3.   I trust that, particularly in the period prior to the
 Secretary of State's visit to Moscow, any plans for exploiting
 the Penkovsky papers will take full account of the political
 factor as well as of their obvious propaganda advantages.


DISTRIBUTED TO:
Northern Dept.
I.R.D.
J.I.A.D.
P.U.S.D.
Security Dept.




MMMMM                      CONFIDENTIAL
```

Soviet warning against the use of the Penkovsky papers by the BBC. *FO 371/182816*

was posted to London to head KGB operations throughout Britain. Over a two year period, he passed over hundreds of classified documents to his handlers during meetings at a Bayswater safe house in West London. In 1985, he came under suspicion and was ordered back to Moscow. Gordievsky was interrogated for several weeks, but no hard evidence could be found to convict him. Unable to guarantee his safety, MI6 took the decision to exfiltrate Gordievsky from the country. He was told to board a train to the Finnish border, where he was met by two British agents and smuggled across the border in the boot of a car. Once across the border, the success of the operation was theatrically announced by the opening strains of *Finlandia* by Sibelius playing loudly on the car stereo.

— 282

SECRET 3

CC 38 (68)

SECRET

Oversea Affairs
Czechoslovakia
(Previous
Reference:
CC (68) 37th
Conclusions,
Minute 2)

1. *The Foreign Secretary* said that we did not know the strength of the Warsaw Pact forces that had invaded Czechoslovakia on the night of 20th–21st August, but it was clear that their grip on the country was complete although some free radio stations were still operating. Ground forces of the Soviet Union, East Germany, Poland and Bulgaria were involved together with Soviet air forces. There were also indications of an increased level of activity in the Soviet long-range air and rocket forces but these did not appear to be in a high state of alert. A remarkable feature of the political situation was that no Czech leader had so far shown himself willing to act as a Soviet puppet. Mr. Dubcek, the Secretary of the Czech Communist Party, and others were in detention, but President Svoboda had issued a statement on the previous evening calling for the withdrawal of the invading troops and for the liberalisation programme in Czechoslovakia to continue; it might be, however, that the Soviet authorities hoped that he would be prepared to co-operate with them. The Czech people were behaving with very great restraint and, although there had been some deaths, widespread bloodshed did not seem likely. It was not clear why the Soviet Union had resorted to military action, despite the agreement reached at Bratislava; it might be that they did not consider that censorship was being sufficiently rigidly imposed by the Czech Government as a result of the agreement or that they feared the outcome of the elections for the Presidium of the Czech Communist Party which were due to take place on 9th September.

Cabinet paper reporting the Soviet invasion of Czechoslovakia . *CAB 128/43*

During the Cold War, obtaining intelligence on the deployment and operational effectiveness of Warsaw Pact forces was a major goal for NATO military planners. The British presence in West Berlin, 100 miles behind the Iron Curtain, proved an invaluable asset. A state-of-the-art listening post located on an artificial hill enabled British intelligence services to listen into the radio traffic of the Warsaw Pact. American and British intelligence services also tunnelled underneath East Berlin and tapped into important telephone wires. The UK mission was officially known as the British Commanders-in-Chief's Mission to the Soviet Forces in Germany (BRIXMIS). It was established in 1946 under international agreement and called for the reciprocal exchange of liaison missions in order to foster good working relations between the military occupation authorities in the two zones. BRIXMIS maintained an official residence in Potsdam, East Germany, but its headquarters and operational centre were located in the Olympic Stadium complex in West Berlin. The Soviets enjoyed reciprocal rights and established a SOXMIS group with its headquarters located in the British zone in Bad Salzuflen, ten kilometres from Herford.

The primary role of BRIXMIS was to monitor the deployment and capability of Warsaw Pact forces. This was achieved by mapping the location of regiments and air fields, including details of the latest equipment, military plans and battle-readiness. The majority of intelligence was gathered using a three-man liaison team that was permitted to travel freely throughout East Germany in designated vehicles under the terms of the agreement. These tours were always followed and harassed by East German security forces. The result was a game of cat and mouse, in which the British vehicles sped off hoping to evade their minders; collisions, crashes and car chases were a common feature of the tours. In rare cases, the encounters ended in serious accidents with a number of individuals ending up in hospital with broken arms and legs.

Intelligence was also gained by more covert means. This included breaking into military depots to measure the dimensions of tank barrels and composition of armour plating, crawling next to runways to photograph missiles and radar equipment as the aircraft took off and entering live fire training areas to recover unexploded ordnance. In one memorable operation, the jet engines of a Soviet fighter were smuggled back to Farnborough for inspection after the aircraft crashed into a lake near Berlin. The mission also had access to two Chipmunk trainer aircraft that were based at RAF Gatow and used for low level photographic reconnaissance. At its height, BRIXMIS produced over 200 reports a year which often supplemented intelligence gathered from other sources. Following the fall of the Berlin Wall and the reunification of Germany in 1990, the mission was deactivated. The end of the Cold War led to a reappraisal of intelligence operations and a search for new roles in an uncertain world.

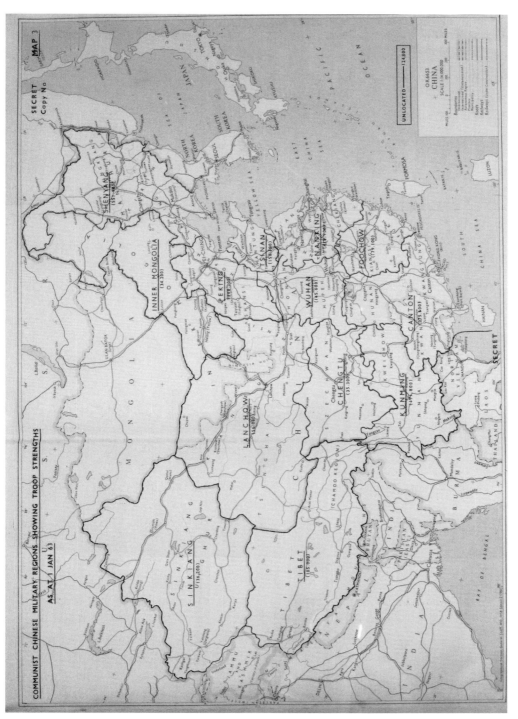

JIC Report: size and deployment of Chinese army, 1963. *CAB 158/48*

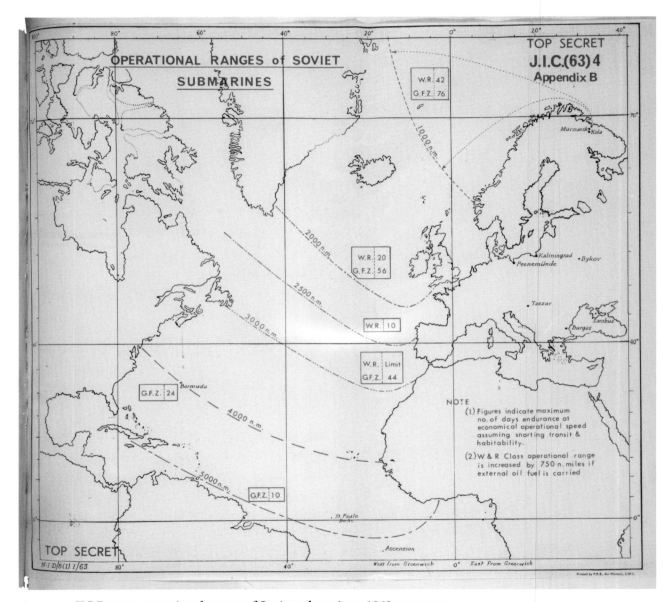

JIC Report: operational ranges of Soviet submarines, 1963. *CAB 158/48*

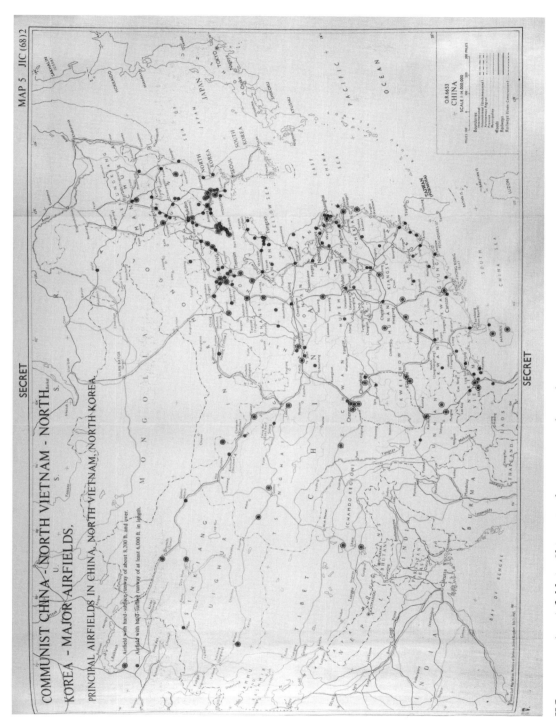

JIC report: major airfields in China, North Vietnam and North Korea. *CAB 158/68*

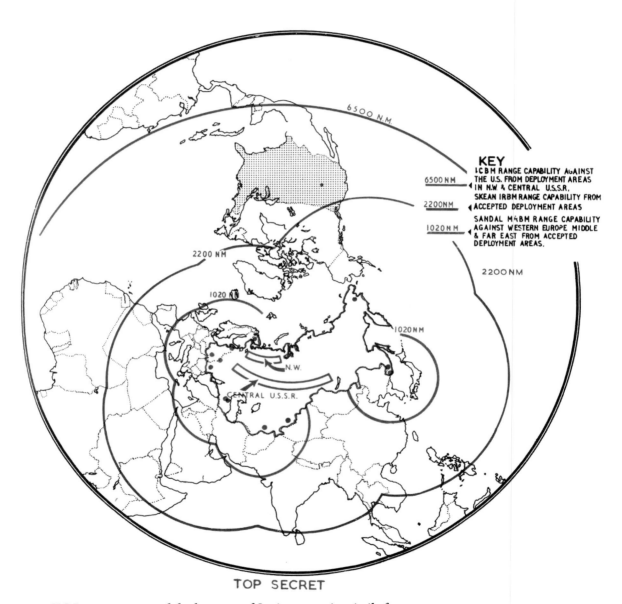

JIC Report: range and deployment of Soviet strategic missile forces. *CAB 158/68*

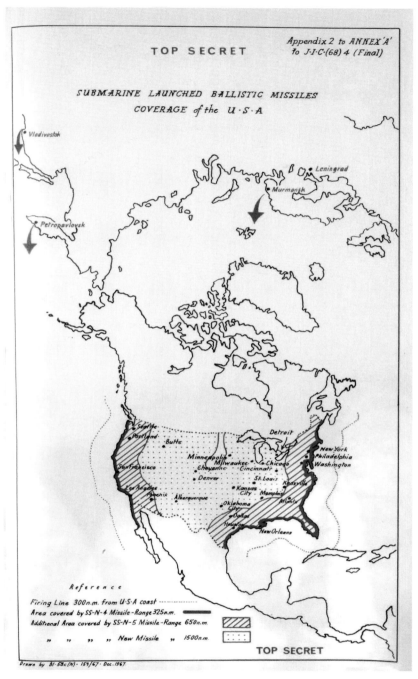

TOP SECRET

JIC Report: vulnerability of the USA to attack from Soviet submarine launched ballistic missiles. *CAB 158/68*

BRIXMIS Quarterly Report: Two Soviet Air Force MiG-17Fs flying over East Germany, March 1966. *WO 208/5248*

BRIXMIS Quarterly Report: Soviet Air Force MiG-17F flying over East Germany, March 1966. *WO 208/5248*

BRIXMIS Quarterly Report: Soviet MAZ 543 Scud missile at the annual October parade in East Berlin, October 1969. *WO 208/5261*

BRIXMIS Bi-Annual Report: Soviet Air Force MiG-21 fighter at Retzow East Germany, May 1971. *WO 208/5266*

BRIXMIS Bi-Annual Report: Soviet Army T-62 tank fitted with a mine plough, East Germany, July 1971. *WO 208/5267*

BRIXMIS Quarterly Report: Soviet MiG 15 fighter, February 1966. *WO 208/5248*

BRIXMIS Quarterly Report: Soviet T-55 tank, 1966. *WO 208/5250*

BRIXMIS Quarterly Report: Soviet Yak-28I tactical bomber, East Germany, 1967. *WO 208/5251*

BRIXMIS Quarterly Report: FROG-5 short range artillery rocket, July 1969. *WO 208/5260*

Soviet Tu-95D Bear over the North Atlantic, April 1970. *AIR 28/1838*

FARMER B 30th January

FISHBED D 30th January

East German FISHBED C/E 20th January

East German FISHBED D 23rd March

East German MIDGET 20th January

Soviet HIPS

BRIXMIS Quarterly Report: various Soviet fighters and helicopters, 1970. *WO 208/5262*

GOING UNDERGROUND: CIVIL DEFENCE

The development of the atomic bomb presented British military planners with momentous challenges. A small, densely populated island, Britain was the ideal target for atomic attack. It was estimated that if a bomb, comparable in size to the weapon that destroyed Hiroshima, was detonated over a typical British city the result would be 50,000 dead, 30,000 homes destroyed with a further 35,000 made uninhabitable. In a future war, a surprise attack with nuclear weapons aimed at major urban areas would eliminate Britain from the conflict. To guard against such an attack, Britain adopted a dual strategy. First, to deter an attack from occurring in the first place, Britain developed a stockpile of nuclear weapons and a modern bomber force capable of mounting a retaliatory strike. Second, to protect the population, more resources were devoted to civil defence and the dispersal of industry. In the aftermath of the Blitz, it was believed that the British population would be able to cope with a limited nuclear strike so long as preparations were in place to protect the public, maintain morale and avoid a panic evacuation of British cities.

To take these plans forward, the government announced its intention to create a civilian volunteer organization to mobilise resources and assume control of the local area in the aftermath of a conventional or nuclear attack. Initial estimates placed the number of full time volunteers required at 168,000. It was also assumed that the urban population would make use of Second World War shelters but most were derelict, decommissioned or unsuitable for public use. Plans to use deep level shelters in the underground proved complex and costly. It was estimated that to construct an adequate shelter system to protect the population would require the country's entire output of steel for the next three years. Unable or unwilling to provide sufficient funding, the government scaled back its civil defence plans. The advice given to the public reflected this position. In the event of attack, the public was told to stay at home and wait for the emergency services to respond.

The government's plans were set out in the Civil Defence Act of 1948 which established the Civil Defence Corps (CDC) and other related services including the Auxiliary Fire Service and the National Hospital Service Reserve. To join the Corps, volunteers had

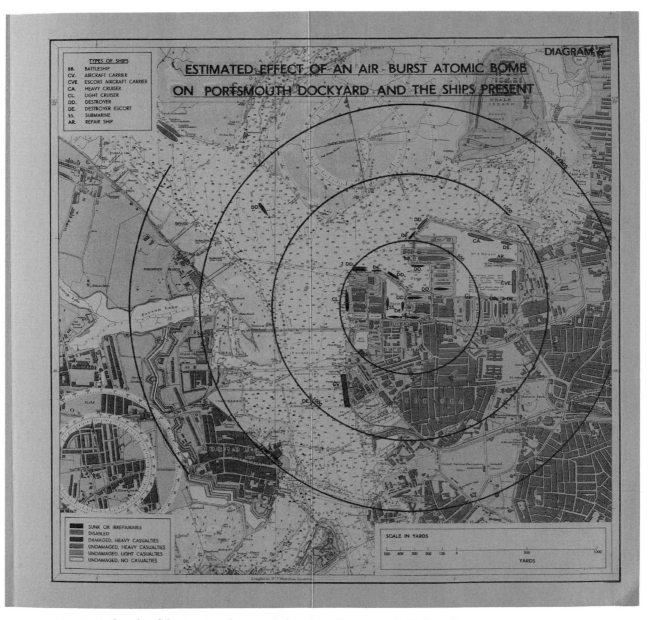

Estimated scale of destruction by atomic bomb on Portsmouth dockyard. *ADM 234/584*

to be aged over 18 if they were women or over 40 if men. The age difference reflected the fact that men over 18 were expected to be called up for military service in the event of war. The CDC was administered at local level by county boroughs and consisted of five operational sections: headquarters, welfare, warden, ambulance and rescue. Overall policy was the responsibility of the Home Office, which issued regulations and ensured local authorities possessed viable plans. Initially, the training of the CDC volunteers was based on a pattern established during the Second World War. This was later updated

to take account of problems posed by nuclear, biological and chemical warfare. To provide practical training, two Civil Defence Colleges were established at Sunningdale in Berkshire and Easingwold in Yorkshire.

Despite the government's best endeavours, the numbers volunteering to enrol in the Civil Defence Corps remained low. To attract new volunteers, a national recruitment campaign

Left: **Civil Defence poster.** *INF 2/122*

Below left: **Civil Defence poster.** *INF 13/236*

Below right: **Civil Defence poster.** *INF 13/326*

was launched in April 1950. The posters and advertisements focused strongly on patriotism and duty. The campaign coincided with the outbreak of the Korean War and saw recruitment increase significantly, with 100,000 joining in the nine months up to 31 March 1951. A further boost to recruitment occurred in 1952, when the age restrictions on men joining the Corps were relaxed allowing anybody over 18 to join, providing they were not due to be called up for military duty. To modernise the organization, a glossy magazine called *Civil Defence* was published, which helped to spread the activities of the Corps to a wider audience. By March 1956, the Civil Defence Corps had 330,000 personnel in its ranks.

The development of the thermonuclear hydrogen-bomb in the mid-1950s revolutionised civil defence. The destructive power of the first US tests were 2,000 times greater than the

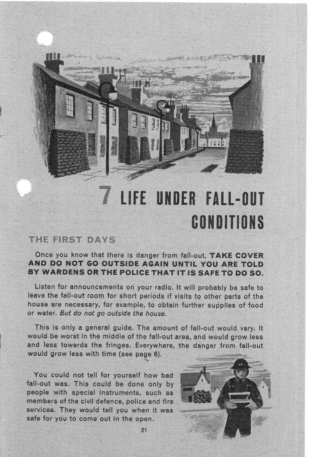

Civil Defence booklet. *HO 338/57*

weapon used over Hiroshima and questioned the very concept of nuclear survival. The consequences of a H-bomb attack were starkly revealed in a top secret report written in 1955 by Sir William Strath, a senior government official. The report estimated the effects of a 10 megaton weapon detonated over London. It concluded that without preparations, 12 million people would die immediately, with a further 13 million trapped in their homes with little hope of rescue. The explosion would result in a crater one mile across and 150 feet deep with radioactive fallout making normal life impossible. The report was so shocking it was kept secret for over fifty years. For many, the hydrogen bomb rendered civil defence redundant. The most significant response came from Coventry, a city largely destroyed by bombing during the Second World War. In a show of defiance, the town council refused to continue with its civil defence plans, believing they were a waste of time and money. The fear of nuclear destruction fuelled support for protest groups such as the Campaign for Nuclear Disarmament who challenged the perceived benefits of civil defence believing that abolition of nuclear weapons was the only way to avoid Armageddon.

The realisation that nuclear war would completely devastate London led officials to consider how government would function in the aftermath of a nuclear attack. In peacetime, the Prime Minister's official residence at 10 Downing Street and the Cabinet Office in Whitehall served as the focus of government in London. These facilities allowed the Prime Minister to be in direct contact with government departments, foreign heads of state and a network of secret underground military operations rooms. In time of crisis, London was expected to be a major target for a Soviet nuclear strike. To provide a secure location for the continuance of central government outside London, the Prime Minister authorised the construction of a Central Government War Headquarters (CGWHQ). The facility was given the codename Turnstile and was constructed 120 feet below ground in a former stone quarry near Cosham in Wiltshire. The CGWHQ had two declared functions: to act as seat of government in the period of survival and reconstruction; and to be an alternate centre to London for authorising nuclear retaliation.

Completed in August 1962, the underground command post extended over thirty-five acres and was capable of accommodating 4,000 people for a period of three months in complete isolation from the outside world. The complex was equipped with a hospital, canteen, laundry and bakery. To provide communication to the outside world, the underground site was provided with its own telephone exchange and a BBC studio from which the Prime Minister could address the nation. Drinking water was supplied from an underground lake and treatment plant. To provide the necessary electricity to operate the complex, four industrial generators were installed which also powered the air conditioning and ventilation plant that was needed to filter out radioactive contamination. To cater for the influx of people expected to work at the CGWHQ, massive amounts of furniture, canteen equipment and stationery were purchased and stockpiled underground including 4,600 mattresses, 2,000 tables, 1,500 boxes of biscuits, 400 typewriters and 12 tea trolleys.

The Hydrogen Bomb poster. *INF 13/281*

Plan of Turnstile nuclear bunker. *CAB 196/74*

CONFIDENTIAL CONFIDENTIAL

13/1

List of Goods held in Supplies Division Stores at Spring Quarry, Corsham.

Item	No.	Item	No.
Bedsteads	250	2 drawer Cabinets	250
2 tier Bunks	1925	4 drawer Cabinets	100
Mattresses	4600	Steel cupboards	100
Blankets	12300	Wood racks	115
Sheets	15340	Kitchen tables	12
Pillows	4600	Food Bins	48
Pillow cases	6500	Tea trolleys	12
Bedspreads	310	Canteen tables	225
Mats	4000	Food trolleys	5
Towels	5125	Weighing Machines	4
Lockers	4260	Dust Bins	24
Tables	2065	Galvanised bottles	16
Tubular arm chairs	550	Boxes of Rations	6000
Fold flat chairs	9085	Boxes of Biscuits	1500
Paper trays	2120	Dental Stores, instruments and equipment	*
Ash trays	2000		
Waste paper bins	2000	Hospital Stores and equipment	*
		Medical stores including Drugs and medicines, ointments, bandages etc.	

* Insufficient for original requirement,
remaining items to be brought in by Army.

CONFIDENTIAL

List of supplies for Turnstile. *CAB 196/75*

To maintain the secrecy of the site, it was considered essential that those government officials selected for work at the CGWHQ would only be informed in the last few days before war was declared. To achieve this, chosen staff were given a printed pass informing them that they had been selected for duty at an important wartime headquarters and that they may be away from home for at least four weeks. Staff were told to return home immediately, pack a small suitcase and return to work. It was further stipulated that only immediate family relatives should be informed. Once back in the office, the selected staff would be bused to Kensington (Olympia) railway station where a special train would take them to a check point located at Warminster, ten miles south of the CGWHQ. Before embarking on the final step of the journey, selected staff would be split up into small teams, briefed on their future role and then driven to the main site aboard an army lorry. The Prime Minister and the Chiefs of Staff were expected to remain at Downing Street until the last moment, before being flown to Turnstile by helicopter.

In addition to the survival of central government, plans were put in place to provide emergency services and maintain order at local level. The plan called for the creation of thirteen civil defence regions, ten in England and one each for Wales, Scotland and Northern Ireland that had responsibility for directing services and helping survivors on the ground. In 1956, the Home Office issued a specification for a network of bunkers capable of resisting nuclear attack, with space for 300 staff and linked to communications systems such as the BBC. Provisions were stockpiled with the bunkers expected to operate for several months if required. The civil defence regions were controlled by Regional Commissioners who had supreme power over local military commanders and could use force, including the shooting of looters, as they saw fit. All the branches of central government were represented in the Regional Seats of Government. It was noted, without apparent irony, that the Inland Revenue would not have any real function in the survival period. In the late 1960s, following a defence review, the RSG network and the CDC were disbanded with contingency planning for civil emergencies devolved to local authorities.

Another volunteer organization that assisted the armed forces during the Cold War was the Royal Observer Corps (ROC). The ROC had been established in 1925 to identify and report sightings of enemy aircraft over UK airspace. During the Second World War, the ROC proved instrumental in tracking German bombers during the Battle of Britain and directing fighters to intercept and destroy V-1 flying bombs. The development of powerful new radar systems following the war meant that the ROC's primary role of identifying and tracking enemy aircraft was no longer necessary. In 1957, the ROC was re-organised to form part of the United Kingdom Warning and Monitoring Organisation (UKWMO) under the control of the Home Office. The purpose of the UKWMO was to support the civilian and military authorities during a nuclear attack by providing information on the location and

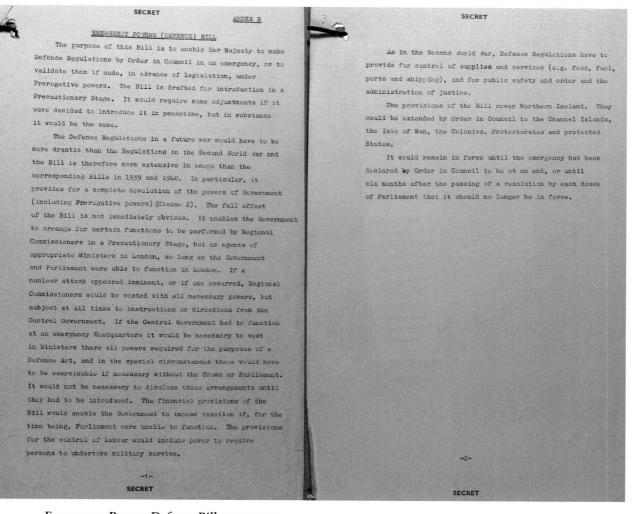

SECRET

ANNEX B

EMERGENCY POWERS (DEFENCE) BILL

The purpose of this Bill is to enable Her Majesty to make Defence Regulations by Order in Council in an emergency, or to validate them if made, in advance of legislation, under Prerogative powers. The Bill is drafted for introduction in a Precautionary Stage. It would require some adjustments if it were decided to introduce it in peacetime, but in substance it would be the same.

The Defence Regulations in a future war would have to be more drastic than the Regulations in the Second World War and the Bill is therefore more extensive in scope than the corresponding Bills in 1939 and 1940. In particular, it provides for a complete devolution of the powers of Government (including Prerogative powers) (Clause 2). The full effect of the Bill is not immediately obvious. It enables the Government to arrange for certain functions to be performed by Regional Commissioners in a Precautionary Stage, but as agents of appropriate Ministers in London, so long as the Government and Parliament were able to function in London. If a nuclear attack appeared imminent, or if one occurred, Regional Commissioners would be vested with all necessary powers, but subject at all times to instructions or directions from the Central Government. If the Central Government had to function at an emergency Headquarters it would be necessary to vest in Ministers there all powers required for the purposes of a Defence Act, and in the special circumstances these would have to be exercisable if necessary without the Crown or Parliament. It would not be necessary to disclose these arrangements until they had to be introduced. The financial provisions of the Bill would enable the Government to impose taxation if, for the time being, Parliament were unable to function. The provisions for the control of labour would include power to require persons to undertake military service.

-1-

SECRET

SECRET

As in the Second World War, Defence Regulations have to provide for control of supplies and services (e.g. food, fuel, ports and shipping), and for public safety and order and the administration of justice.

The provisions of the Bill cover Northern Ireland. They could be extended by Order in Council to the Channel Islands, the Isle of Man, the Colonies, Protectorates and protected States.

It would remain in force until the emergency had been declared by Order in Council to be at an end, or until six months after the passing of a resolution by each House of Parliament that it should no longer be in force.

-2-

SECRET

Emergency Powers Defence Bill. *DEFE 13/321*

magnitude of an atomic explosion. This data would be combined with weather reports provided by the Meteorological Office to forecast the path and intensity of the radioactive cloud as it drifted across Britain. To allow coverage of the entire country, a network of over 1,500 underground monitoring posts was constructed. Each post was built twenty-five feet below the ground and expected to be occupied by a team of three for a period of between seven and twenty-one days following a nuclear attack. Access to the underground post was achieved by a steel ladder leading to a single room with power provided by a twelve volt battery. Exactly how many volunteers would have shown up for duty in such conditions following a nuclear attack was a matter of speculation.

COPY № ......

CONFIDENTIAL

REGIONAL SEATS OF GOVERNMENT

MANUAL FOR THE GUIDANCE OF STAFF

CONFIDENTIAL

This document is the property of Her Majesty's
Government and is issued for the personal
information of the person to whom it is entrusted
in confidence within the provisions of Section 2
of the Official Secrets Act, 1911, as amended by
the Official Secrets Act, 1920. The recipient is
personally responsible for its safe custody and
for seeing that its contents are disclosed only to
authorised persons.

PREPARED BY THE HOME OFFICE

JANUARY 1965

Regional Seats of Government, manual for staff. *HO 332/315*

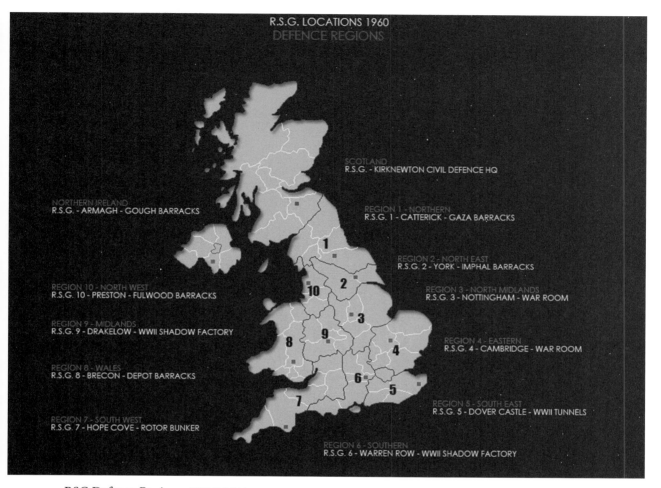

RSG Defence Regions. *TNA Exhibition*

The advent of détente in the 1970s reduced public fears of imminent nuclear war and led to a rundown of civil defence. The rapprochement between the two superpowers was short-lived. In 1979, the Soviet Union invaded Afghanistan and began to deploy increasing numbers of the SS-20 nuclear missile. NATO responded by stationing Pershing and cruise missiles throughout Europe. The deployment coupled with President Reagan's uncompromising rhetoric, in which he likened the Soviet Union to an evil empire, increased the threat of nuclear confrontation. In an attempt to reassure the British public, the government commissioned *Protect and Survive,* a series of booklets, radio broadcasts, and public information films that informed the population on how to protect themselves following a nuclear attack. The thirty page booklet distributed in 1980 contained a series of instructions to be taken by all

Protect and Survive logo.
HO 322/776

households to improve their chances of survival in the unlikely event of nuclear war. This information was supplemented by two further publications: *Domestic Nuclear Shelters*, which contained advice for building a fallout shelter in the home, and *Domestic Nuclear Shelters – Technical Guidance*, that contained various designs for the construction of long-term permanent shelters. The publications were widely criticised as ineffective and unduly alarmist.

Protect and Survive was also adapted for broadcast on television appearing as a series of animated short public information films. The films were the creation of Richard Taylor Cartoons, who also produced the children's animated cartoon series *Crystal Tipps and Alistair* about the adventures of a girl and her pet dog first shown on the BBC in 1971. The same animation techniques were used in the public information films. These conveyed in simple terms the instructions and guidance found in the *Protect and Survive* booklet and provided advice on water consumption, sanitation and dealing with causalities. The series was only intended to be broadcast if the government considered that a nuclear attack was

Protect and Survive booklet, front cover, 1980. *INF 6/2531*

imminent. Some of the recordings were leaked to the press and shown on British television in March 1980 on the BBC current affairs programme Panorama. The BBC also worked with the Home Office to produce a pre-recorded radio announcement that would be broadcast to the nation in the event of nuclear attack. The announcement was to be transmitted on the BBC Wartime Broadcasting Service and read by an authoritative senior BBC journalist. The announcement was intended to be repeated at regular intervals to provide the public with reassurance and advice. The script recently released at The National Archives informed listeners to stay in their homes and that the number of casualties and the extent of the damage were not yet known. Further information would be provided as soon as possible. The draft of a speech to be delivered to the nation by the Queen in the event of nuclear war was also released.

Foreword

If the country were ever faced with an immediate threat of nuclear war, a copy of this booklet would be distributed to every household as part of a public information campaign which would include announcements on television and radio and in the press. The booklet has been designed for free and general distribution in that event. It is being placed on sale now for those who wish to know what they would be advised to do at such a time.

May 1980

If Britain is attacked by nuclear bombs or by missiles, we do not know what targets will be chosen or how severe the assault will be.

If nuclear weapons are used on a large scale, those of us living in the country areas might be exposed to as great a risk as those in the towns. The radioactive dust, falling where the wind blows it, will bring the most widespread dangers of all. No part of the United Kingdom can be considered safe from both the direct effects of the weapons and the resultant fall-out.

The dangers which you and your family will face in this situation can be reduced if you do as this booklet describes.

Protect and Survive booklet, forward, 1980. *INF 6/2531*

In 1990, following the end of the Cold War, all further work on government bunkers and civil defence infrastructure was suspended. In July 1991, the Home Secretary announced that civil defence plans needed to reflect the realities of the international situation and that government planning would now be based on the assumption that three months' advance notice would be given rather than the current seven days. The Royal Observer Corps was stood down and the UKWMO disbanded. In December 2004, the Central Government Wartime Headquarters at Corsham was decommissioned and put up for sale. Promotional material produced for the sale suggested that the deep shelters would make the ideal location for a secure data vault or wine cellar. In March 2013, in recognition of its historic role during the Cold War, the underground telephone exchange and radio studio were placed on the Heritage at Risk Register run by Historic England. In its reasons for designation, it was stated that the site was of supreme importance during the Cold War and an unparalleled example of Britain's national military heritage.

A-Frame nuclear shelter diagram, 1985. *HO 322/1073*

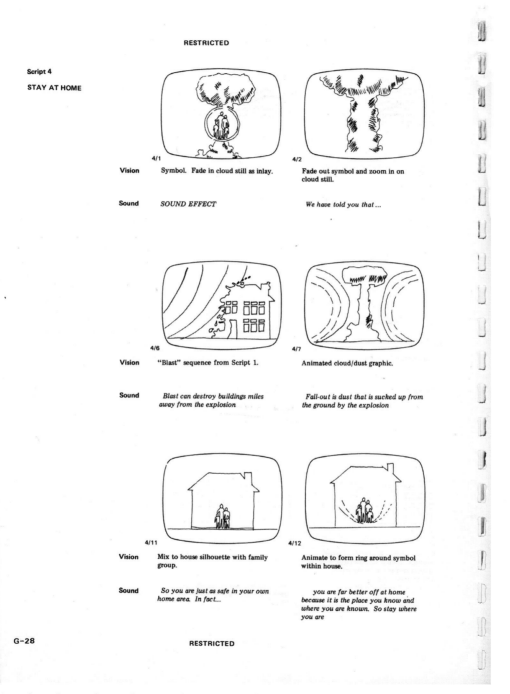

RESTRICTED

Script 4

STAY AT HOME

4/1

Vision	Symbol. Fade in cloud still as inlay.
Sound	*SOUND EFFECT*

4/2

Vision	Fade out symbol and zoom in on cloud still.
Sound	*We have told you that ...*

4/6

Vision	"Blast" sequence from Script 1.
Sound	*Blast can destroy buildings miles away from the explosion*

4/7

Vision	Animated cloud/dust graphic.
Sound	*Fall-out is dust that is sucked up from the ground by the explosion*

4/11

Vision	Mix to house silhouette with family group.
Sound	*So you are just as safe in your own home area. In fact...*

4/12

Vision	Animate to form ring around symbol within house.
Sound	*you are far better off at home because it is the place you know and where you are known. So stay where you are*

RESTRICTED

Storyboard page for nuclear attack protection film. *HO 322/776*

SECRET

THIS DOCUMENT IS THE PROPERTY OF HER BRITANNIC MAJESTY'S GOVERNMENT

MISC 93(83) 31   COPY NO   60

4 March 1983

CABINET

WINTEX-CIMEX(83) COMMITTEE

———

EXERCISE   EXERCISE   EXERCISE

Text of a Message to the Nation broadcast by
Her Majesty The Queen at Noon on Friday 4 March 1983

****

When I spoke to you less than three months ago we were all enjoying
the warmth and fellowship of a family Christmas. Our thoughts were
concentrated on the strong links that bind each generation to the ones
that came before and those that will follow. The horrors of war could
not have seemed more remote as my family and I shared our Christmas joy
with the growing family of the Commonwealth.

Now this madness of war is once more spreading through the world and
our brave country must again prepare itself to survive against great odds.

I have never forgotten the sorrow and pride I felt as my sister and I
huddled around the nursery wireless set listening to my father's inspiring
words on that fateful day in 1939. Not for a single moment did I imagine
that this solemn and awful duty would one day fall to me.

We all know that the dangers facing us today are greater by far than at
any time in our long history. The enemy is not the soldier with his rifle
nor even the airman prowling the skies above our cities and towns but
the deadly power of abused technology.

But whatever terrors lie in wait for us all the qualities that have helped
to keep our freedom intact twice already during this sad century will once
more be our strength.

1

SECRET

125

Speech for Queen Elizabeth II in the event of nuclear war, 1983, page 1. *CAB 130/1249*

SECRET

My husband and I share with families up and down the land the fear we feel for sons and daughters, husbands and brothers who have left our side to serve their country. My beloved son Andrew is at this moment in action with his unit and we pray continually for his safety and for the safety of all servicemen and women at home and overseas.

It is this close bond of family life that must be our greatest defence against the unknown. If families remain united and resolute, giving shelter to those living alone and unprotected, our country's will to survive cannot be broken.

My message to you therefore is simple. Help those who cannot help themselves. give comfort to the lonely and the homeless and let your family become the focus of hope and life to those who need it.

As we strive together to fight off the new evil let us pray for our country and men of goodwill wherever they may be.

God Bless you all.

****

EXERCISE   EXERCISE   EXERCISE

2

SECRET

Speech for Queen Elizabeth II in the event of nuclear war, 1983, page 2. *CAB 130/1249*

CHAPTER 5

FIGHT THE POWER: THE PROTEST MOVEMENT

The 1950s witnessed a significant growth in the stockpile of nuclear weapons possessed by the two superpowers. By 1955, the US atomic stockpile was estimated at 2,400 nuclear weapons with the Soviet Union possessing just 200 warheads. New and more advanced weapons, including the hydrogen bomb, were also being developed. To examine the military effects of nuclear weapons and formulate new designs, the US established a dedicated test site in Nevada and a site in the Pacific Ocean close to the Marshall Islands. These early tests were all conducted above ground with dangerous levels of radiation released into the environment. In 1954, a US hydrogen bomb test conducted in the Pacific resulted in a large amount of radioactive nuclear fallout. Islands nearby were contaminated, with the inhabitants suffering from radiation sickness and increases in cancer rates and birth defects. A Japanese fishing boat, the inappropriately named *Lucky Dragon,* sailing eighty miles from the test site was enveloped by the radioactive cloud. The crew suffered acute radiation sickness, with the boat's chief radio operator later dying from his injuries. It was feared that the radioactive fish they had been carrying had entered the Japanese food supply.

The increase in nuclear testing led to public disquiet over the dangers associated with radiation and the long term effect of exposure to radioactive particles in the atmosphere. In his 1954 Easter address, Pope Pius XII called for the prohibition of nuclear weapons and an immediate end to atmospheric tests. In Britain, concern over nuclear weapons and atmospheric testing led to the creation of the Campaign for Nuclear Disarmament (CND) which held its first public meeting in February 1958 at Central Hall, London. The meeting was attended by 5,000 people with speakers including the philosopher, Bertrand Russell, the historian A.J.P. Taylor and the Labour politician Michael Foot. The policy platform adopted by CND was unequivocal and called for the immediate and unconditional renunciation of nuclear weapons by the British government coupled to reductions in conventional armed forces. It further demanded that Britain halt its nuclear test programme and close all American air bases located in the UK that could be used by US nuclear forces.

To announce its arrival, CND organised a number of demonstrations. The most visible was the 1958 Aldermaston march which took place over the Easter weekend during which 3,000 people marched from Trafalgar Square in London to the Atomic Weapons Research Establishment at Aldermaston in Berkshire, a distance of 55 miles. In the summer of 1958, CND organised a mass lobby of Parliament attended by 7,500 people. This was followed by a women's conference 'Women against the Bomb' which highlighted the medical, scientific and moral dangers associated with atomic weapons and nuclear war. To underscore the moral imperative of nuclear disarmament, a Christian CND movement was established under the direction of the Reverend John Collins, a former chaplain in the Royal Air Force during the Second World War and Canon of St Paul's Cathedral in Central London.

The formation of CND represented a widespread fear and opposition to nuclear weapons and harnessed the desire of the younger generation for a peaceful and egalitarian world. In 1960, popular opposition to nuclear weapons led the Labour Party to adopt a resolution at its annual party conference calling for unilateral nuclear disarmament. The policy was opposed by the leader of the Labour Party, Hugh Gaitskill, who succeeded in reversing the decision the following year. This set back, disillusioned many anti-nuclear protesters and resulted in a rejection of the parliamentary process in favour of direct action. A vocal supporter of direct action was Bertrand Russell, the CND president who resigned from the organization to form the Committee of 100. The new grouping was a shadowy organization composed of activists who disagreed with the leadership's consensual approach. They soon adopted a radical agenda advocating mass nonviolent resistance and civil disobedience to force the government to change its policy. Its first action was a sit-down demonstration at the Ministry of Defence in London in February 1961, to protest against the stationing

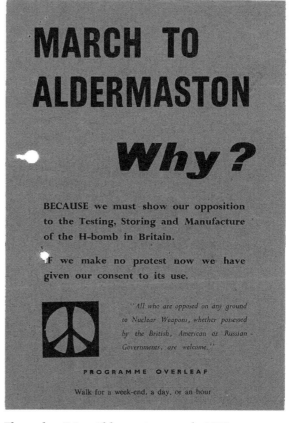

Flyer advertising Aldermaston march, 1958. *HO 325/149*

of US Polaris submarines at Holy Loch in Scotland. This was followed by protests outside the US and Soviet embassies and a mass sit down in Trafalgar square that blocked traffic for most of the day.

The apparent success of the protests emboldened several activists to undertake direct action at four RAF bases located at Brize Norton, Ruislip, Wethersfield and Cardiff. The demonstrators planned to cut through the perimeter fences and stage a sit down protest on the runway, preventing aircraft from taking off or landing. These plans soon came to the attention of the police and security services who arrested the ringleaders and charged them with conspiracy and incitement to breach the Official Secrets Act. Those arrested included Michael Randle, the secretary of the Committee of 100 and Patrick Pottle, a founding member of the organization. Randle and Pottle were later found guilty and sentenced to eighteen months in prison for their part in organising the direct action at RAF Wethersfield. During his time in prison, Randle struck up a friendship with George Blake, the notorious Soviet agent, and became involved in one of Britain's most audacious prison escapes.

Born in Rotterdam in 1922, Blake was a former British agent who had been recruited by MI6 and posted to Berlin where he was tasked with recruiting East German agents. In 1961, Blake was sentenced to forty-two years imprisonment for passing secret information to Moscow. Randle considered the length of sentence imposed on Blake outrageous and agreed to help him escape. In October 1966, Randle, together with Patrick Pottle and Séan Bourke, a petty criminal from Limerick in Ireland, acquired a walkie-talkie and a rope ladder with rungs made from knitting needles. On a signal from Randle, the ladder was thrown over the wall allowing Blake to make good his escape. Following his break out, Blake stayed at various 'safe' houses around London rented by friends of Randle and Pottle. Blake finally made his escape from the country by hiding in a secret compartment in a camper van which was driven to Eastern Europe by Randle. The van also contained Randle's two children to distract any curious customs officers who might be tempted to check the inside of the van. Blake later settled in the Soviet Union and remained unrepentant over his betrayal of British agents. In 2007, he was awarded the Order of Friendship by Russian President Vladimir Putin. Randle and Pottle later stood trial at the Old Bailey for their part in the escape, but the jury acquitted them on all counts.

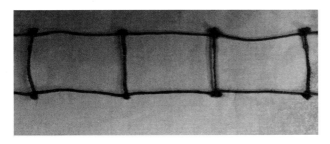

Rope ladder made from knitting needles used in the escape of George Blake 1966. *HO 278/7*

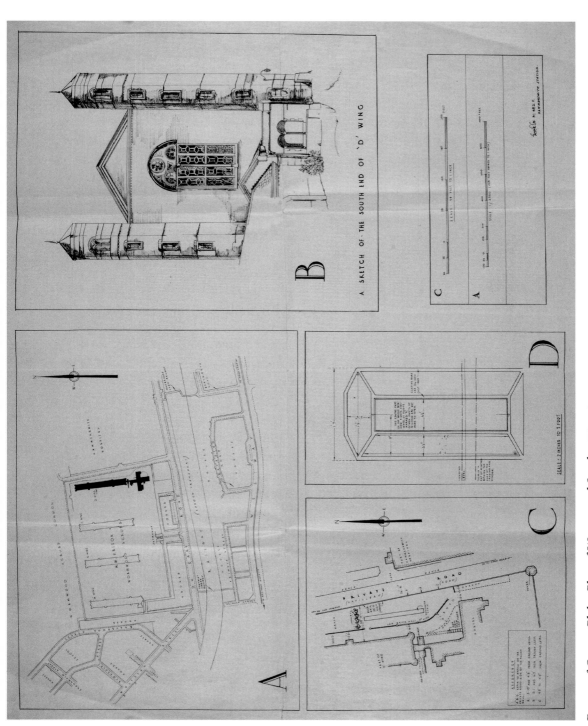

Escape of George Blake, Plan of Wormwood Scrubs. *HO 278/7*

A further organization associated with the anti-nuclear movement was the Spies for Peace network, a loose anarchist grouping with links to the Committee of 100. In 1963, the 'Spies' achieved notoriety by breaking into a secret government bunker at Warren Row near Reading and copying a number of classified documents. The bunker was the Regional Seat of Government (RSG-6) for the South East of England, one of a network from which the country would be administered in the event of nuclear war. Built to accommodate over 300 staff, the RSGs were responsible for the maintenance of law and order in their region and organising reconstruction work in the aftermath of a nuclear exchange. The location and purpose of the RSGs was classified and consequently unknown to the general public. Spies for Peace subsequently published the information they had obtained from the bunker in a pamphlet, *Danger! Official Secret RSG-6*. In April 1963, 3,000 copies of the pamphlet were sent out to carefully chosen MPs, the national press and peace activists and later distributed on CND's Easter march to Aldermaston. Several people were arrested, although the original 'Spies' were never identified or caught.

In the late 1960s and 1970s, the focus of the peace movement shifted away from nuclear weapons with attention directed towards opposing the war in Vietnam and demonstrating against American imperialism. It was only in the early 1980s following the breakdown in East-West relations that fear of nuclear conflict once again became a major factor in the growth

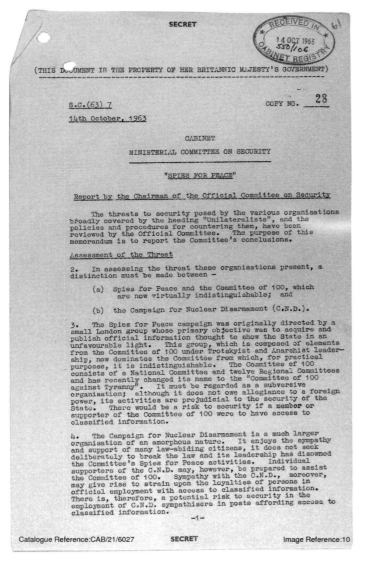

Report on 'Spies for Peace' for the Government's Security Committee.
CAB 21/6027

E.R.

DRAFT

SECRET

✓ 69

PRIME MINISTER

I have considered with my colleagues in the Ministerial Committee on Security the threat to security posed by supporters of "Spies for Peace" and other unilateralist organisations who are employed in the public service or in defence industry.

The threat is a real one, as was shown by the disclosures about the Regional Seats of Government, and any further such disclosures could not only be nationally damaging — they could also be highly embarrassing politically. I think it would therefore be as well, if you agree, that I should reported orally to the Cabinet on the Committee's conclusions.

There is much that can and will be done under existing security arrangements to counter the threat from the unilateralists and to exclude such people, when judged appropriate, from secret work. The Security Service are extending their coverage of the more extreme organisations and their supporters. The present assessment is that our arrangements should prove adequate.

It may later be found necessary to extend our arrangements by giving Departments the same authority to take overt action to remove Trotskyists and Anarchists from secret work as they now have to remove Communists and Fascists; and, if so, the view of the Committee was that we should not shrink from it. But such an extension of our present arrangements would need to be announced publicly, which would have the effect of giving the unilateralist organisations a status and prestige they do not deserve. The Committee concluded that we ought not to take this step until we find that it is necessary; and that for the present we should continue to rely on existing security arrangements.

SECRET

Catalogue Reference:CAB/21/6027

Image Reference:9

Letter to the Prime Minister detailing the actions of 'Spies for Peace'. *CAB 21/6027*

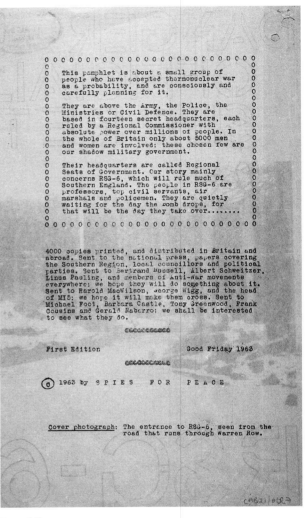

Above left: RSG-6 pamphlet produced by 'Spies for Peace' front. *CAB 21/6027*

Above right: RSG-6 pamphlet produced by 'Spies for Peace' inside cover. *CAB 21/6027*

of the peace movement. The impetus behind the resurgence of the anti-nuclear movement was NATO's decision to station Pershing and cruise missiles in Europe in response to the Soviet deployment of the SS-20 missile. Huge anti-nuclear marches were held throughout Western Europe and Britain to protest against the deployment of Pershing and cruise. In London, a protest rally attracted 250,000 marchers, the largest ever mass demonstrations in the UK up to that time. Membership of CND leapt from 3,000 in 1980 to 50,000 in less than a year. The protest movement divided the main political parties. Many Labour local authorities declared themselves nuclear free zones. The Conservative Party established Youth for Multilateral Disarmament which campaigned against CND's policy of unilateral disarmament, seeking instead to eliminate nuclear weapons by gradually reducing the stockpiles held by all sides.

In September 1981, a women's march from Cardiff arrived at Greenham Common US Air Force base in Berkshire, where cruise missiles were to be stationed. The women set up a peace camp and chained themselves to the perimeter fence. The peace camp soon became a focus of protest and a symbol of resistance against nuclear weapons. In December 1982, 30,000 women joined hands around the base at the *Embrace the Base* event. A year later, 70,000 protestors

What is Unilateral Disarmament?

Unilateral disarmament means just one country giving up nuclear weapons without any others doing so. It is one-sided disarmament. Some people believe the UK should do this to 'set an example'.

Why does this support the Soviet Union

The Soviet Union is a Communist dictatorship where there is no real freedom. It is constantly attempting to expand, for example into Angola, Mozambique, Cambodia, Ethiopia, Afghanistan. It is opposed to the sort of freedoms we are used to in Britain. If Britain put down its weapons the Russians wouldn't copy us, they would laugh at us. There would be nothing to stop them invading us like they invaded Afghanistan.

Who supports one-sided Disarmament?

Not surprisingly all the extreme Left-wing political parties such as the Communist Party and the Socialist Workers Party.

The real way to peace - World Disarmament

If peace is really to be achieved then all countries must disarm. Britain must keep its nuclear weapons to use as a bargaining counter with the Russians. It would be stupid to throw away our negotiating cards.
The Government should make it quite clear to the Russians we want to talk peace and achieve multi-lateral disarmament. But we can only do that from a position of strength.

- -
If you would like to join or receive further information about Youth for Multilateral Disarmament please complete:

Name _____
Address _____

Please send me membership details ☐ further information ☐
and post to: **YOUTH FOR MULTILATERAL DISARMAMENT** 1a Whitehall Place, London SW1

Published by Youth for Multilateral Disarmament, 1a Whitehall Place, London SW1
Printed by O & I Print, 104 Northgate Street, Gloucester, England.

The government has a Christmas present for you

Tell them you don't want it

Southwark
a nuclear free zone

Above left: **Youth for Multilateral Disarmament, leaflet.** *FCO 46/2744*

Above right: **Nuclear Free Zone poster, Southwalk.** *BS 20/98*

formed a human chain linking the base at Greenham Common to Aldermaston and the weapons facility at Burghfield. The government was concerned that the presence of peace camps at Greenham Common could be used as cover by enemy agents to gain access to the air base. The cruise missiles were eventually removed from the base in 1991, following the signature of the Intermediate-Range Nuclear Forces Treaty. The peace camp remained in place until 2000 and became a focus of protest against the Trident nuclear programme. The decision to replace Polaris with Trident missiles was announced in 1980. Soon afterwards, a peace camp was established at the Faslane submarine base to protest against the stationing of nuclear weapons in Scotland. In October 1988, three anti-nuclear demonstrators were apprehended after forcing their way into the base and gaining entry into the nuclear deterrent submarine HMS *Repulse*. Two further intruders were arrested inside the onshore oil depot. During the incident, anti-nuclear graffiti was daubed in the control room of HMS *Repulse*.

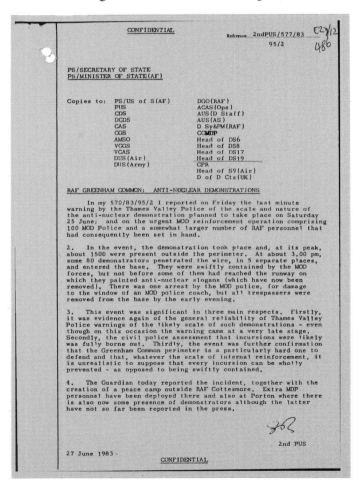

Despite the best endeavours of the anti-nuclear protest movement, Britain has retained its nuclear arsenal with a commitment to reduce the overall nuclear weapon stockpile to no more than 180 warheads by the mid-2020s. Public support for unilateral disarmament has remained fairly constant at twenty-five per cent of the population reaching a peak of thirty-one per cent in September 1982. The retention of a minimum nuclear deterrent still enjoys majority public support within Britain. Since the end of the Cold War, the number of states possessing nuclear weapons has increased from five to nine. The drive to halt the proliferation of nuclear weapons has become a major goal of international diplomacy. The primary focus of the peace movement has now shifted to environmental concerns,

Report on Greenham Common anti-nuclear demonstrations. *DEFE 34/3020*

with opposition against nuclear power and global warming emerging as significant aspects of the political debate. Whether Britain will continue to possess a nuclear deterrent for the remainder of the twenty-first century is a question that has yet to be fully resolved.

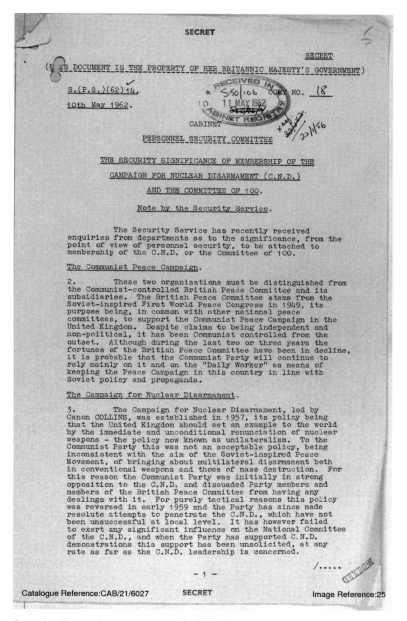

Security Committee report on the British Peace Committee and CND.
CAB 21/6027

SECRET 2A

*File No
cc Sir P.C.
COGA2D*

10 DOWNING STREET

LONDON SW1A 2AA

From the Private Secretary

12 October 1988

CLYDE SUBMARINE BASE: INTRUSION

You wrote to me on 10 October about the intrusion by anti-nuclear demonstrators into the Clyde Submarine Base at Faslane.

The Prime Minister is absolutely appalled by this incident. She thinks it has all the hallmarks of slackness in protecting sensitive defence installations of which there has been far too much evidence, despite all the assurances which she has received from the Ministry of Defence about the measures taken to provide protection. She wishes a full report to be made to her at the earliest possible moment with a clear indication of where responsibility lies, what action is being taken against those responsible for such a grave breach and recommendations to ensure that it does not happen in future. I should be grateful if you would let me know very rapidly when we can expect such a report.

CHARLES POWELL

Brian Hawtin, Esq.,
Ministry of Defence.

SECRET

Intrusion into Clyde submarine base by anti-nuclear protesters, Prime Minister's response.
PREM 19/2615

CONFIDENTIAL

1.   The Cabinet were informed of the business to be taken in the House of Commons during the following week.

2.   THE FOREIGN AND COMMONWEALTH SECRETARY said that the speech by the First Secretary of the Soviet Communist Party Mr Andropov on 21 December 1982, followed by the Warsaw Pact Declaration of 5 January 1983, had focussed public opinion on arms control issues. The right public response for the West was to maintain pressure for the zero option; to identify those elements in the Warsaw Pact offer which were positive while pointing out the flaws and inadequacies; to ensure that the substance was properly considered in the negotiations in Geneva on intermediate range nuclear forces (INF); and only when this had been done to pronounce on the merits. There was no prospect of the Soviet Union accepting the zero option, as had been made clear once again during the recent visit to Bonn by the Soviet Foreign Minister, Mr Gromyko; but it remained important to press for it. A solution which fell some way short of the zero option would be worth having provided that, as the Prime Minister had emphasised in the House of Commons, it reflected a true balance and was based on genuine figures. The United States Administration had kept the British Government fully informed about the course of the INF negotiations, including the private talks which Mr Nitze, the United States chief negotiator, had had with his Soviet opposite number in Geneva during the summer. At the moment there was some disarray in Washington following the rejection by the Congress of President Reagan's proposal to deploy MX missiles and the difficulties which had arisen over the defence budget. The forthcoming visit to the United Kingdom of the United States Vice-President, Mr. Bush, which would focus on nuclear issues, would therefore need particularly careful handling. The latest developments highlighted the importance of the domestic debate about deployment to the United Kingdom of American ground-launched cruise missiles (GLCMs). This was a "hearts and minds" operation. Opinion polls suggested that public opinion was basically sound, but the campaign to put the Government's policies across to the public needed to be moved into higher gear.

In discussion it was pointed out that supporters of the Campaign for Nuclear Disarmament (CND) and the Peace Movement were likely to create problems for public order out of proportion to their numbers, and that this was an increasing cause of concern to Chief Constables. Protests were likely to focus on GLCM deployment but would cover the whole range of nuclear issues, civil as well as military. The forthcoming debate in the Church of England Synod on the Bishop of Salisbury's working group report on "The Church and the Bomb" could have an important impact on public opinion: a large number of the younger clergy were against nuclear weapons. On the other hand recent public opinion polls showed that 72 per cent of the electorate were against Britain relinquishing its nuclear deterrent as long as other countries retained their nuclear weapons; and reactions to a recent television debate between Mr John Selwyn Gummer MP and the secretary for CND, Monsignor Bruce Kent, had shown that the public overwhelmingly endorsed the Government's policies when these were effectively presented. Another recent opinion poll had shown a significant increase in public concern about defence issues; but the reasons for this required further analysis, which was in hand.

THE PRIME MINISTER, summing up the discussion, said that the Government had an excellent case and a majority of the public was sympathetic to it. It was important that all members of the Government should present that case as vigorously and effectively as possible.

1
CONFIDENTIAL

21

Cabinet express concern over influence of CND. *CAB 128/76*

CHAPTER 6

AFRICA: PROXY WARS

In its early stages, the Cold War was confined primarily to the divided continent of Europe, where the armed forces of NATO and the Warsaw Pact faced each other in a nuclear stand-off. The deadlock in East-West relations was reflected in the United Nations, with both sides seeking to build alliances to support their respective positions. In the mid-1950s, the Non-Aligned Movement was formed. Primarily composed of the newly independent countries of the third world, its member states sought to remain neutral in the struggle between the major powers and establish an independent path in world politics based on peaceful co-existence and mutual respect for each other's territorial integrity and sovereignty. From its inception, the movement had differing political and ideological perspectives; some members believed that the fight against colonialism and imperialism was paramount, while others sought to rebuild their economies and improve trade. As the Cold War intensified, both the Soviet Union and the United States sought to expand their influence within Asia and Africa by offering to support national liberation movements and providing much needed development aid and military assistance. The Cold War was now global and would be fought out in a series of proxy wars carried out in the paddy fields and jungles of Asia, the deserts and scrubland of the Middle East and the savanna and forests of Africa.

At the end of the Second World War, the African continent underwent rapid decolonisation as many countries gained their independence from European powers. In March 1957, Ghana (formerly the Gold Coast) became the first sub-Saharan African country to gain its independence from Britain. With the exception of Southern Rhodesia, Britain's remaining colonies in Africa were all granted independence by 1968. The colonial possessions of France, Belgium and Portugal in Africa underwent similar transformations. The rapid withdrawal of European powers from the continent created political instability and the emergence of rival factions and militias. The Soviet Union and the United States sought to exploit the power struggle in Africa by providing money, arms and political cover to friendly governments and political parties who promised to support them in the Cold War struggle. The Soviets and their allies lent their support to a variety of Marxist national liberation movements with the West supporting anti-communist forces. The provision of diplomatic and military aid allowed both sides to expand their influence in Africa at the expense of the other. The resultant conflicts, military coups and armed rebellions destabilised the region and led to the deaths of thousands of civilians due to famine, sickness and war.

One of the first battle grounds was the Democratic Republic of Congo (formerly Zaire) which had been a Belgian territory since 1885. Life for the indigenous Congolese under Belgian rule was harsh, with many dying from poverty, sickness and hazardous working conditions. Resistance to Belgian rule began in the 1950s. A key role was played by the *Mouvement National Congolais* (MNC). Established in 1956, the MNC sought to transcend tribal allegiances and create a unitary and centralised Congolese nation. Its leader was Patrice Lumumba, who soon established the MNC as the most dominant party in the Belgian Congo. In 1960, the Congo achieved independence, becoming the Republic of Congo-Léopoldville with Lumumba as Prime Minister. The new government sought to consolidate power and soon began to outlaw opposition parties and jailing their leaders. This heavy handed approach led to the secession of the mineral rich province of Katanga, under the leadership of Joseph Mobutu, the army chief of staff and staunch anti-communist. The central government in Léopoldville sought to crush the rebellion but was denied western support. Lumumba turned instead to the Soviet Union who willingly supplied him with weapons and scores of military advisors.

The involvement of Moscow worried officials in Washington as the Congo contained the world's largest deposits of uranium ore, some of which had been used in the atomic bomb detonated over Hiroshima. The Americans were determined to deny the Soviets access to the uranium mines and plotted with Mobutu to remove Lumumba from power. On 14 September 1960, Mobutu led a successful coup, suspending parliament and arresting Lumumba. The Soviets demanded his immediate release. They further called for the removal of UN peacekeeping forces from the country and the detention and trail of Mobutu on charges of sedition and inciting the army to rebellion. In January 1961, Lumumba and his key lieutenants were taken to Katanga, imprisoned and executed by firing squad. It was falsely reported that Lumumba and two other prisoners had escaped from prison. His death was finally announced over Katangan radio in February. The official communique stated that he had been killed by angry villagers after escaping from prison and threatening the inhabitants. The US continued to support Mobutu, who ruled the country, which remained firmly in the pro-western camp, until his death in 1997. It was speculated that the assassination of Lumumba was planned and carried out by western intelligence. In 1975, the US Senate found that while the CIA had conspired to kill Lumumba, it was not directly involved in the murder. Lumumba's death was also investigated by the Belgian authorities. The report published in 2001 concluded that although the Belgium government had not ordered his elimination, Lumumba's execution was carried out by a firing squad led by a Belgian Captain.

189

SECRET   3

C.C. 43 (60)

Congo Republic.
(Previous Reference:
C.C. (60) 42nd Conclusions, Minute 2.)

1. *The Foreign Secretary* said that the Prime Minister of the Congo Republic, Mr. Lumumba, had threatened to accept an offer of military assistance by the Soviet Union unless the United Nations called on all Belgian forces to withdraw from the Congo within three days. The Assistant Secretary-General of the United Nations, who was in the Congo, had rejected this ultimatum and had said that if the Soviet Union's offer were accepted, the United Nations forces would be withdrawn. Although it was not likely that Mr. Lumumba would carry out his threat, the possibility of some Soviet intervention in the Congo could not be excluded. It remained our aim to ensure that all aid to the Congo was channelled through the United Nations, but that the United Nations forces did not intervene in the Katanga as long as law and order were maintained there. It would be in our interests if the United Nations could play some mediatory role in achieving a settlement between the Congo Republican Government and the Katanga Government which preserved the provincial rights of Katanga and safeguarded Western interests in that area. It was satisfactory that the Prime Minister of the Federation of Rhodesia and Nyasaland had now made a statement that it was not possible in the constitutional circumstances for the Federation to meet the request of the provincial Premier of Katanga for military assistance.

The Cabinet—
    Took note of this statement by the Foreign Secretary.

Soviet Union.
(Previous Reference:
C.C. (60) 9th Conclusions, Minute 3.)

2. *The Prime Minister* said that he proposed later in the day to announce to Parliament the terms of the note which was to be presented to the Soviet Government rejecting the accusation that a United States aircraft, based in the United Kingdom, had violated the territory of the Soviet Union on 1st July and had in consequence been shot down over Soviet territorial waters. In addition to this formal reply, he would also inform Parliament of the terms of a personal letter which he had sent to Mr. Khrushchev at the same time, in which he expressed his anxiety about the way in which the world situation was developing. He hoped that this message would show that, while the British people would not be separated from their Allies by threats or propaganda, they sincerely desired a relaxation in world tension.

The Cabinet—
    Took note with approval of this statement by the Prime Minister.

Government Expenditure.
(Previous References:
C.C. (60) 7th Conclusions, Minute 4, and
C.C. (59) 57th Conclusions, Minute 5.)

3. The Cabinet had before them a memorandum by the Chancellor of the Exchequer (C. (60) 113) on estimates of Government expenditure for the years 1961–62 and 1962–63.

The Chancellor of the Exchequer said that the latest forecasts showed that Government expenditure for 1961–62 would show an increase of more than £200 millions over the current year, and that there would be a further increase of £100 millions in the following year. On a realistic assumption about pay rates, it would be wise to envisage additions to these increases of at least £50 millions for 1961–62, and of £100 millions for 1962–63. The forecasts were based on existing commitments, and took no account of a considerable number of substantial projects which would involve still further extra expenditure. If all these projects were accepted, supply expenditure in 1961–62 would be £381 millions more than in the current year— an increase of 7·9 per cent.; and in 1962–63 there would be a further

SECRET

'7660—2   B 2

Cabinet informed of Soviet arms supplies to the Congo Republic. *CAB 128/34*

LUMUMBA AND THE COMMUNISTS

There is a growing volume of evidence which indicates that both before and after the declaration of Congo Independence, Patrice Lumumba and his closer colleagues were working with outside Communists (in Belgium) as well as with Communist advisers and agents in the Congo.

For some time the Soviet bloc had made determined efforts to infiltrate the Congo; even before plans for its independence were announced the Communists had a leading figure in Leopoldville in the person of Dr. Josef Virrius, Czech Consul-General and later Ambassador to the new republic.

Virrius became closely acquainted with Congolese political leaders such as Lumumba and Antoine Gizenga: he acted as a liaison between world Communism and Congolese politicians who appeared useful material.

As a result of the activities of Dr. Virrius the M.N.C. established contact with the Belgian Communist Party (P.C.B.). Thus when Lumumba attended the Congo Constitutional Conference in Belgium he, and a number of his supporters (Gizenga, Bisukiro, Ilunga, Kashamura and Mwamba) developed these contacts. Lumumba himself attended a meeting of the Liege branch of the Belgian Communist Party in February.

During this meeting Lumumba arranged with Albert Goyen, a militant Belgian Communist, for a supply of election-eering equipment. He also had a number of meetings at the same time with Albert Deconinck, a member of the Politbureau of the Belgian Communist Party, responsible for the direction of the "colonial" section of the Party.

Following his contacts in Belgium, Lumumba arranged for a number of his supporters (Nguvulu, Mandungu and Belenge) to attend the XIII Congress of the Belgian

Soviet involvement in the Congo. *FCO 168/69*

In February 2002, the Belgian government issued a formal apology to the Congolese people for involvement in the events that led to the death of Lumumba.

Congo's independence and the success of its liberation movement had immediate consequences for its southern neighbour Angola. A Portuguese colony since 1834, the people of Angola soon began to demand independence. The main political party was the Union of the Peoples of Angola which was first established in 1954 to fight against Portuguese domination of the country. In 1962, it merged with the Democratic Party of Angola,

57

SECRET   7

C.C. 7 (61)

Government were not proposing to accept. The statement would then become an announcement of Government policy, without specific reference to the Templer Report.

In discussion the point was made that it was known that a Committee had been appointed to consider this problem and that there was some public interest in its outcome. The Commonwealth Secretary said that, even so, he believed that he could deal with this matter in Parliament without disclosing the substance of the Committee's recommendations.

The Cabinet—

Authorised the Commonwealth Secretary to announce in Parliament, without reference to the Report of the Templer Committee, the Government's decision incorporated in the draft statement annexed to C. (61) 3.

Congo
Republic
(Previous
Reference:
C.C. (61) 5th
Conclusions.
Minute 1)

8. *The Foreign Secretary* reported the latest developments in the Congo. The Soviet Government had reacted very strongly to the news of Mr. Lumumba's death, and they must now be expected to do their utmost to strengthen the position of Mr. Gizenga. They might try to persuade some of the countries which had military forces in the Congo to put them at Mr. Gizenga's disposal, but in this they were not likely to be successful. Alternatively they might themselves try to provide him with arms and supplies by means of an air-lift to Stanleyville. The United States Government had asked us to consider what could be done to forestall such a manoeuvre. Meanwhile the Soviet Government were intensifying their efforts to undermine the position of the Secretary-General of the United Nations. Their communications to the organisation were now being sent, not to the Secretary-General, but to a Russian member of the secretariat.

In the Cabinet's discussion special emphasis was laid on the importance of preventing the establishment of a Soviet air-lift into Stanleyville. It was suggested that the Chiefs of Staff might be asked to prepare a technical appreciation of the difficulties which the Russians would encounter in organising such an air-lift. The Foreign Secretary should also consider whether it would be practicable for United Nations forces in the neighbourhood to create such obstructions as would deny the use of the airfield to the Russians. The Secretary-General of the United Nations would presumably be justified in instructing United Nations forces to take passive steps to prevent unilateral intervention in the Congo by any foreign Power.

The Cabinet—

Took note that the Foreign Secretary would consider, in consultation with the Minister of Defence, what steps it would be practicable to take to prevent the organisation of a Soviet air-lift into Stanleyville; and that, in the light of this, he would consider whether the Secretary-General of the United Nations could properly be pressed to instruct United Nations forces in the area to take action to this end.

Cabinet Office, S.W. 1.
16th February, 1961.

SECRET

Soviet reaction to the death of Lumumba.
CAB 128/35

to become the National Liberation Front of Angola (FNLA). The organization received the tacit backing the United States which was keen to see a pro-American and anti-Soviet organization succeed the Portuguese colonial administration. The FLNA was led by Holden Roberto, a brother in law to Joseph Mobutu. It also had a military wing with training camps based in the Congo. The liberation struggle was joined by two other armed groups. The first was the People's Movement for the Liberation of Angola (MPLA) which was founded in 1956. This was an avowedly Marxist organization which enjoyed the active support of the Soviet Union and Cuba. The second was the Union for the Total Independence of Angola (UNITA) which was formed in 1966 by Jonas Savimbi, who had split from the FNLA and later established close ties with the United States.

2.   THE FOREIGN AND COMMONWEALTH SECRETARY said that the Popular Movement for the Liberation of Angola (MPLA), with Soviet and Cuban support, were now clearly getting the upper hand in the Angolan fighting. As many as 12,000 Cubans were now in Angola or on the way there. The South Africans were disengaging: they had of course never admitted their involvement. The American Secretary of State, Dr Kissinger, had made no headway in his efforts to persuade the Soviet Union to withdraw their support from the MPLA. The Soviet Ministry of Foreign Affairs had told our Ambassador that their intervention had been at the request of the MPLA whom they had long supported. They saw no reason not to continue to do so. The South Africans could take no comfort from the indecisive outcome of the Council of the Organisation of African Unity since those African States which had not recognised the MPLA were likely to change their stance one by one before very long. Although a government composed of the three factions in Angola, for which he had hoped, was now unlikely, he still hoped that the MPLA might see the wisdom of forming a government of national reconciliation, including some representatives of the tribes which had opposed them, since military victory would otherwise not end their problems. Our own policy should be to continue low level contacts with the MPLA, and to go on pressing publicly for the withdrawal of all external forces. He had considered several times the possibility of raising the issue in the United Nations Security Council but had decided that it would be unwise to do so against the express wish of the African Governments who, with the exception of Zaire, had unanimously opposed United Nations involvement in the dispute. We had to recognise that many African States must now be feeling insecure under the impact of what, in East/West terms, could only be regarded as a major Soviet success. There would also be repercussions on the Chinese position in Africa which had been built up with great skill but would now be weakened; this was already heightening the dispute between China and the Soviet Union. The only ray of hope was that, if the MPLA finally prevailed, other African Government's would subsequently put pressure on the MPLA for the withdrawal of the Russians and Cubans.

The Cabinet -

1.   Took note of the statement by the Foreign and Commonwealth Secretary.

Angola, strength of the MPLA. *CAB 128/58*

The first uprising began in March 1961, when armed rebels mounted an incursion into northern Angola from bases in the Congo. Encountering little resistance, the insurgents burnt down government outposts and trading centres and killed a significant number of government officials. The civilian population was also targeted, with terrified villagers taking refuge in the forests or fleeing inland. The government in Portugal reacted quickly to the insurgency and deployed two battalions of troops to the region. The Portuguese forces mounted a series of military reprisals which resulted in the deaths of 20,000 Angolan civilians. The international community was appalled at the level of destruction. In June 1961, the United Nations Security Council declared Angola a non-self-governing territory and called on Portugal to desist from repressive measures against the Angolan people. The resolution was approved by China, the United States, the Soviet Union and all the non-permanent members, with France and the United Kingdom abstaining. The conflict continued throughout the 1960s with guerrilla attacks mounted by the MPLA, FLNA and UNITA. The rival factions often fought each other and received varying degrees of support from the Soviet Union, China and the United States. The Angolan war became increasingly unpopular in Portugal due to its drain on resources and the strains it placed on diplomatic relations with other western nations.

In April 1974, the political landscape of Angola changed dramatically following a military coup in Lisbon which overthrew the right-wing government headed by Marcelo Caetano. The coup was led by the Armed Forces Movement composed of junior military officers opposed to the regime. It was soon joined by a popular civil resistance campaign. The revolution led to the fall of the government and the end of almost 50 years of authoritarian rule in Portugal. One immediate consequence of the revolution was the withdrawal of Portuguese administrative and military personnel from its overseas colonies in Africa. Angola was granted independence on 11 November 1975, following negotiations with the transitional Portuguese government. The agreement called for the integration of the three military wings of the Angolan parties into a single unified army. Political disagreements soon emerged, with the MPLA, backed by the Soviet Union and Cuba, seeking to establish sole control over the entire country. Violent clashes between the three militias quickly intensified with the MPLA forcing the FLNA and UNITA forces out of the major cities and towards the country's southern border with Namibia.

The success of MPLA forces began to concern Angola's neighbours, particularly South Africa, who feared the imposition of a Marxist state on its northern border. The United States' administration was also determined to prevent the Soviet Union establishing a military base that would directly threaten western interests on the African continent. To stop MPLA forces from taking complete control of the country, the South African government deployed 2,000 troops to support FLNA and UNITA forces, with the CIA supplying over $30 million in covert aid. The introduction of South African forces had immediate results, with the FLNA and UNITA forces gaining control of five provincial capitals. In response to the military reverse, the Cuban government sent 18,000 troops to support the MPLA fighters. The Jugoslav navy also deployed two warships off the coast of Angola to assist Cuban forces. The introduction of Cuban troops proved decisive and allowed the MPLA to consolidate its hold on power. The Angolan civil war was a major battle ground in the Cold War, with the Soviet Union, Cuba and other Eastern bloc nations providing support for the MPLA government. The People's Republic of Angola was declared on 11 November 1975.

Portugal's decision to withdraw its forces from the continent had immediate consequences for the Portuguese colony of Mozambique on Africa's east coast. A major source of gold and ivory, the country had been under Portuguese control since 1505. Following the Second World War, the indigenous population increased their demands for self-determination and an end to colonial rule. In 1962, the Front for the Liberation of Mozambique (FRELIMO) was established, with the aim of freeing the country from Portuguese rule. Formed in exile in Tanzania, FRELIMO was a Marxist organization and advocated the armed struggle as the key to victory. FRELIMO fighters received training and weapons from the Soviet Union, East Germany and China and began a military campaign, ambushing Portuguese patrols, railroad lines and colonial outposts from bases located deep in the bush. By the late 1960s, one fifth of the country was in FRELIMO hands with approximately 8,000 insurgents fighting Portuguese forces. Following the 1974 coup, the new government in Lisbon called for a ceasefire. Negotiations with FRELIMO resulted in the signing of the Lusaka Accord in September, 1974. The country's independence was announced on 25 June 1975. FRELIMO soon established a one-party state and outlawed all opposition. The country quickly descended into a long and violent civil war between FRELIMO and the anti-Communist Mozambican National Resistance (RENAMO). The opposition forces were supported by Rhodesia and South Africa who viewed a Marxist Mozambique as a direct challenge to their continued survival. Following the end of the Cold War, FRELIMO and RENAMO signed the Rome General Peace Accords, ending the Mozambique civil war.

The decolonization of Africa by western powers left Rhodesia and South Africa as the only two states on the continent that were governed by white minority regimes. There was fear that the victory of national liberation movements would inspire the black population of Rhodesia and South Africa to intensify their struggle and demand majority rule. The liberation movement in Rhodesia was divided between two main parties. The Zimbabwe African People's Union (ZAPU) under the leadership of Joshua Nkomo and the Zimbabwe African National Union (ZANU) led by Robert Mugabe. The leadership of ZAPU was based in Zambia and received support from the Soviet Union and Cuba. ZANU had its headquarters in Mozambique and was heavily dependent on China and other communist countries for finance, arms supplies and training. Together ZANU and ZAPU formed the 'Patriotic Front' and began a bush war to remove the minority government led by Ian Smith of the Rhodesian Front. The liberation struggle placed the West in a difficult position.

INWARD SAVING TELEGRAM

FROM DAR ES SALAAM TO COMMONWEALTH RELATIONS OFFICE

By Bag   CRO/FO/WH DISTRIBUTION

Mr. Fowler
No. 28 Saving   D. 22 February, 1965
20 February, 1965

        Addressed to C.R.O. telegram No. 28 Saving of
20 February
Repeated for information Saving to:
        Lourenço Marques   Lisbon   POMEC Aden
        Washington   Zomba   Lusaka
        Nairobi   Kampala

        Following Communique (No. 11 in series begun in December)
was issued by FRELIMO H.Q. in Dar es Salaam on 17 February.

                Mozambique Liberation Front

        In the last two weeks of January our military force
made a fierce attack and sabotage.

1.   On the 16th of January, 1965 one storehouse belonging
to "Cha de Milange", in the district of Zambeze, with much
building material was completely destroyed by our forces.
Two bridges also equally destroyed in the same area.

2.   On the 20th of January 1965, at Mocuba, in Zambeze
district, our combatants ambushed a convoy of three trucks.
The cars were all destroyed by explosives and 16 Portuguese
soldiers died.

3.   In Cabo Delgado, the military force of FRELIMO made
a surprise attack at the administration station of Muidumbe
where 10 Portuguese soldiers were on guard. Three of them
were killed. On the following day in the same region a convoy
of five trucks was attacked. Two trucks were destroyed and
some soldiers died. Other vehicles managed to escape.

4.   On the 23rd of January one group of FRELIMO members
ambuscaded with homemade rifles in the region of chief
Mbalale. At this popular action 12 Portuguese soldiers were
killed and two were injured. Twelve rifles and ammunition
were captured.

sssss

Military communique issued by FRELIMO. *FO 371/181967*

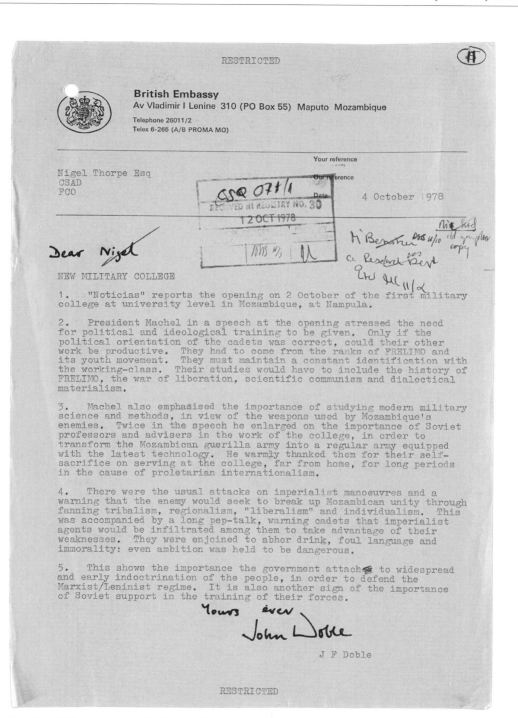

RESTRICTED

British Embassy
Av Vladimir I Lenine 310 (PO Box 55) Maputo Mozambique

Telephone 26011/2
Telex 6-265 (A/B PROMA MO)

Your reference

Nigel Thorpe Esq
CSAD
FCO

Our reference

CSQ 071/1

RECEIVED IN REGISTRY NO. 30
12 OCT 1978

Date   4 October 1978

Dear Nigel

NEW MILITARY COLLEGE

1.   "Noticias" reports the opening on 2 October of the first military
college at university level in Mozambique, at Nampula.

2.   President Machel in a speech at the opening stressed the need
for political and ideological training to be given. Only if the
political orientation of the cadets was correct, could their other
work be productive. They had to come from the ranks of FRELIMO and
its youth movement. They must maintain a constant identification with
the working-class. Their studies would have to include the history of
FRELIMO, the war of liberation, scientific communism and dialectical
materialism.

3.   Machel also emphasised the importance of studying modern military
science and methods, in view of the weapons used by Mozambique's
enemies. Twice in the speech he enlarged on the importance of Soviet
professors and advisers in the work of the college, in order to
transform the Mozambican guerilla army into a regular army equipped
with the latest technology. He warmly thanked them for their self-
sacrifice on serving at the college, far from home, for long periods
in the cause of proletarian internationalism.

4.   There were the usual attacks on imperialist manoeuvres and a
warning that the enemy would seek to break up Mozambican unity through
fanning tribalism, regionalism, "liberalism" and individualism. This
was accompanied by a long pep-talk, warning cadets that imperialist
agents would be infiltrated among them to take advantage of their
weaknesses. They were enjoined to abhor drink, foul language and
immorality: even ambition was held to be dangerous.

5.   This shows the importance the government attaches to widespread
and early indoctrination of the people, in order to defend the
Marxist/Leninist regime. It is also another sign of the importance
of Soviet support in the training of their forces.

Yours ever

John Doble

J F Doble

RESTRICTED

Foreign Office account of Marxist doctrine taught in new Mozambique military college.
FCO 45/2297

On one hand, it supported UN sanctions against Rhodesia, on the other, it sought to contain communist expansion and was reluctant to see the country transformed into a client state of the Soviet Union. The South African government also viewed Rhodesia as an effective buffer state, preventing the establishment of a communist regime on its northern border and provided covert military support.

In 1976, the US and South Africa applied diplomatic pressure on the Rhodesian regime to accept some form of majority rule. It was hoped that an agreed solution would end the guerrilla war and facilitate the emergence of a moderate black leadership. This process led to a settlement with a number of African nationalist parties not involved in the armed struggle.

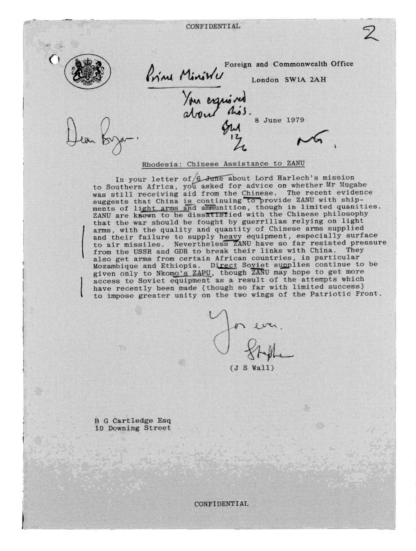

Foreign Office report of Chinese military assistance to ZANU forces in Rhodesia.
PREM 19/107

The main party was the United African National Council which was led by Bishop Abel Muzorewa of the Methodist Church. In the country's first democratic election, held in March 1978, Muzorewa became the first black Prime Minister of Zimbabwe. The settlement was rejected by the 'Patriotic Front' as control of the country's police, armed forces, civil service and judiciary still remained under the control of the white minority. The international community refused to accept the validity of the agreement and the uprising continued. In 1979, in an attempt to reach a comprehensive settlement, the British invited all parties to attend a peace conference at Lancaster House in London. The conference, which lasted three months, led to a ceasefire, followed by internationally supervised elections. These were won by ZANU led by Robert Mugabe. Formal independence was granted to Zimbabwe on 18 April 1980, with Mugabe serving as Prime Minister.

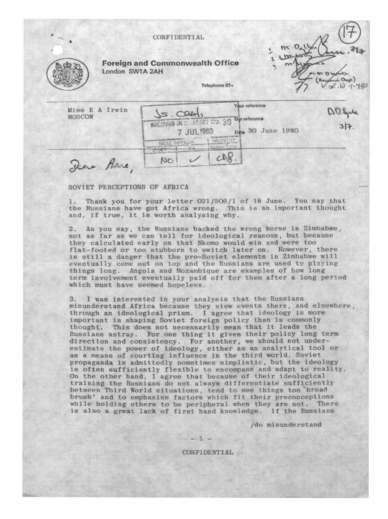

Foreign Office report on Soviet Perceptions of Africa.
FCO 326/58

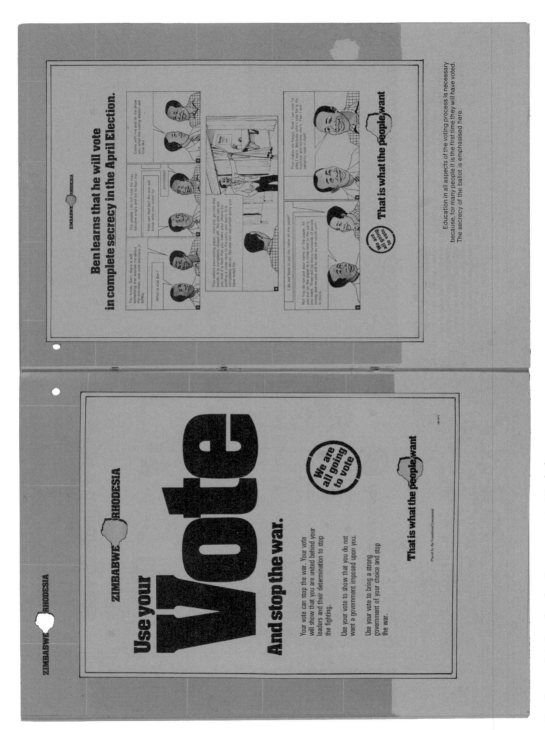

Leaflet explaining the election process in Zimbabwe. *PREM 19/106*

CONFIDENTIAL

Rhodesia VLB

cc HO   D/T
   LCO   CO
   HMT
   MOD
   LPO
   LSO

1O DOWNING STREET

From the Private Secretary

29 May 1979

Rhodesia

Thank you for your letter of 25 May about Lord Harlech's mission to Southern Africa.

The Prime Minister has seen your letter and, with one important exception, is content with the arrangements envisaged for Lord Harlech's consultations. The Prime Minister agrees that Lord Harlech should have talks with President Kaunda, President Nyerere, President Machel, Sir Seretse Khama and General Obasanjo. The Prime Minister does not, however, consider that Lord Harlech should meet the co-leaders of the Patriotic Front. The Prime Minister has commented that she has never done business with terrorists until they become Prime Ministers.

The arrangements foreshadowed in your letter for the announcement of Lord Harlech's mission and for handling publicity have, of course, now been overtaken by the leak of his appointment which occured over the weekend.

I am sending copies of this letter to the Private Secretaries to other members of OD and to Martin Vile (Cabinet Office).

B. G. CARTLEDGE

J. S. Wall, Esq.,
Foreign and Commonwealth Office.

CONFIDENTIAL

Zimbabwe, Prime Minister opposed to talks with the Patriotic Front. *PREM 19/106*

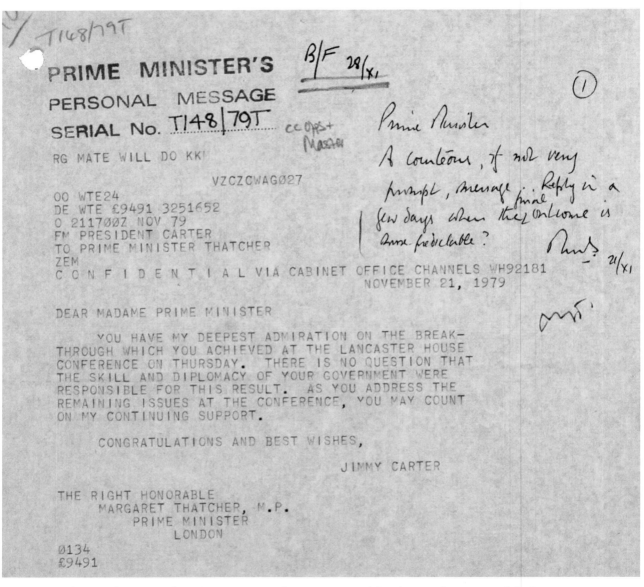

Telegram from President Carter congratulating Margaret Thatcher on the success of the Lancaster House agreement. *PREM 19/115*

The victory of black nationalist forces in Zimbabwe left South Africa as the only remaining minority regime on the African continent. The country was originally colonised by the Dutch and British, and became independent in 1931. South African politics was dominated by Afrikaner nationalism which enforced a system of racial segregation known as apartheid.

CONFIDENTIAL

There ffs give the answer to your query about the Amnesty provisions. Apart policy c OD (79) 40? 28/xi

Ref. A0779

PRIME MINISTER

Southern Rhodesia:　Zimbabwe Independence Bill

(OD(79) 40)

This memorandum by the Foreign and Commonwealth Secretary deals with the policy issues raised by the Zimbabwe Independence Bill which may be required very shortly.　Cabinet on 1st November and OD on 5th November have already touched on the need for an Independence Bill to follow the interim Enabling Bill already passed.　This is the first full exposition of the Independence Bill, including its potentially controversial provisions on citizenship and amnesty.　The Bill cannot be introduced until the Lancaster House conference has concluded, e.g. in the weeks beginning 3rd or 10th December, but will then be very urgent. Legislation Committee agreed on 27th November that it should be given full priority once approved by OD, but unless the conference has secured agreement with the Patriotic Front the Opposition may make it difficult to secure the Bill before the Christmas Recess.

2.　The Bill has been fully discussed at official level between Departments and in view of the urgency it is hoped that it can be agreed by Ministers out of Committee in the course of this week.

3.　Of the potentially controversial aspects the extension by one year of the right of some Rhodesians to register as citizens of the United Kingdom and Colonies should be readily defensible.　The amnesty in United Kingdom law for "political offences" (paragraph 8) and the amnesty in Southern Rhodesian law to be granted by the Governor (paragraph 9) are logical consequences of a settlement and are necessary for elections in Rhodesia.　They should only be controversial if the settlement has not included the Patriotic Front but would then only be facets of the larger row over proceeding with independence in this situation, which OD has already accepted.　(OD(79) 12th Meeting, 5th November.)　The amnesty for sanctions offences (paragraph 10) could be controversial since it cannot equally be seen as necessary to promote reconciliation within Rhodesia.　But it will have been preceded by an announcement of the finding by the Director of Public Prosecutions

This will be very controversial

-1-

Prime Minister's update on the Zimbabwe Independence Bill. *PREM 19/115*

Resistance to apartheid was heavily influenced by the pacifist teachings of Mahatma Gandhi, who had lived in South Africa for over twenty years. The government responded by shooting unarmed demonstrators and banning anti-apartheid parties, including the African National Congress (ANC). The leaders of the ANC were put on trial or fled the country. The resistance went underground and turned to armed struggle and guerrilla warfare. In 1962, Nelson Mandela, a leading member of the resistance was arrested and sentenced to life imprisonment for conspiring to overthrow the state. The brutal suppression of the 1976 Soweto uprising, in which 176 protestors were killed, appalled the international community and strengthened the legitimacy of the ANC both at home and abroad.

During the height of Cold War, many western governments provided tacit support to the South African regime. The justification was the strategic and economic importance of the country. South Africa was strongly anti-communist and situated at the tip of Africa at the juncture of the Indian and Atlantic Oceans. The Royal Navy had use of naval bases in the Cape under the Simonstown Agreement and was able to protect international trading routes. If the West required military assistance on the African continent, it was dependent on South African support as it was the only state in the region that possessed a modern infrastructure, port facilities and airfields. The West was determined that these should not fall into Soviet hands. Economically, the West was reliant on South Africa for supplies of chromium, manganese, uranium and industrial diamonds which were essential raw materials for the industries of Europe and North America. The South African government encouraged this worldview and projected itself as a last bastion of civilization in the fight against communist domination of the African continent.

The collapse of the Soviet Union in 1989 meant that the South African government could no longer use the threat of communism as justification for their continued oppression of the majority black population. There were also consequences for the ANC, who could no longer rely on Moscow or Havana for economic and military support. By the early 1990s, both sides were looking for a political solution to enable a peaceful transition to majority rule. In February 1990, Nelson Mandela was released from prison after spending more than twenty-seven years behind bars. Bilateral negotiations between the South African government led by F.W. de Klerk and the ANC led to the repeal of apartheid legislation, followed by democratic, multiracial elections. In 1993, Mandela and de Klerk were jointly awarded the Nobel Peace Prize. The country's first free elections were won by the ANC, with Nelson Mandela elected South Africa's first black president, a position he held until 1999.

The African continent was a major battleground of the Cold War. The ideological struggle conducted by the two superpowers found fertile territory in the newly independent states of post-colonial Africa. The Soviet Union viewed the various national liberation movements

PASSAGE FOR INCLUSION IN PAPER ON RELATIONS WITH THE THIRD WORLD

4. Soviet policies have suffered a reverse in Zimbabwe with Mugabe's election victory and his decision to follow moderate policies; and with the poor showing in the elections of Mr Nkomo on whom they had pinned their hopes. It is essential for the West to help in the consolidation of these gains, which are, as yet by no means firmly established, and to be alert to the considerable scope which remains for Soviet meddling. Continuing conflict in Namibia permits the Russians to tighten their hold on Angola; to strengthen their links with Zambia, to embarrass the West by forcing them nearer to a decision between their interests in Black Africa and South Africa and to divide the West among themselves. A major black/white row over Namibia could also wreck chances of a modus vivendi between South Africa and Zimbabwe, turn Mozambique back from its present overtures to the West, and kill any chance of early internal reform in South Africa. Thus a Namibia settlement is an important Western aim. The signs are that the Front Line States are also reluctant to see the UN settlement plan break down. The South Africans may now be moving hesitantly towards agreement to implement the plan, and the momentum must be maintained.

Niether in Namibia, nore more generally in Southern Africa, do the Russians want to risk open conflict either with South Africa, or with direct Western interests such as vital mineral supplies or the Cape route. If there is an internationally accepted Namibia settlemen' the Russians will hope that the Africans will launch an all out effort short of war to remove apartheid. A Namibia settlement will give a furthe: breathing space for internal reform in South Africa, and will strengthen the hand of Mr P W Botha against his right wing critics. The West must use every opportunity to demonstrate to South Africa that the communist threat is strengthened by white obduracy and that rapid progress to government by consent is essential. The West needs to be more cohesive in this, refusing to be split by debates over the pace and extent of change in South Africa, and united in its resolve that vital Western interests should not be thrown away in pointless confrontation. There is a need for a concerted Western effort in the Third World to take advantage of post Zimbabwe optimism to put across Western positions.

Foreign Office analysis of Soviet objectives in Zimbabwe and Southern Africa. *FCO 326/58*

as Marxist allies and supported the armed struggle with money and military assistance. The United States regarded the insurgents as terrorists and provided support to anti-communist rebels in an attempt to stop the continent falling under Soviet domination. The result was a series of debilitating and brutal proxy wars which claimed millions of lives and destabilised the African continent, leading to impoverished economies and dictatorial regimes. For the many Africans caught up in these conflicts, their needs and aspirations were considered of secondary importance to the battle of ideas between East and West and remains a lasting and painful legacy of the Cold War.

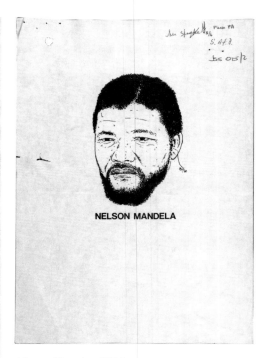

Above: Sketch of Nelson Mandela, 1980. *FCO 105/442*

Left: Foreign Office report into Soviet expansion in the Third World. *FCO 326/58*

CHAPTER 7

THE LAND OF MAKE BELIEVE: COLD WAR CULTURE

The Cold War was not solely a military conflict but also a battle for hearts and minds played out in the plots and storylines of novels and films and the popular pastimes of television, music and sport. The Cold War defined society's innermost hopes and fears and imbued a generation in both East and West with a sense of vulnerability and doubt. Fear and anxiety about nuclear Armageddon fired the imagination of artists. In the communist East, artists, writers and musicians became active participants in the ideological struggle, advancing the values of Soviet patriotism and proletarian internationalism. In the West, values of democracy, individualism and consumerism were brought to life in fictional heroes and Hollywood movies. Science fiction authors explored apocalyptic themes, whilst a significant number of folk and pop songs resonated Cold War tensions and the idealism of the peace movement. Cold War culture also dealt with the dark side of human nature with stories of espionage and surveillance reflecting themes of paranoia and distrust.

In Britain, the value of propaganda was readily appreciated due to its success in the Second World War. This role was undertaken by the Political Warfare Executive, a clandestine body created to produce and distribute propaganda and misinformation with the aim of deceiving the enemy and sustaining morale within occupied countries. These skills were equally applicable to the demands of the Cold War. The British government's principal weapon in the ideological battle against Soviet communism, and its associated front organizations, was the Information Research Department (IRD) of the Foreign Office. Established in 1948, IRD operated both in secret and in the open and fostered strong links, often using intermediaries and non-attributable briefings, with well-known authors, opinion formers and journalists within British society. Its objectives were to disparage the Soviet model of society and to promote the values of liberal democracy and individual freedom.

One of the first writers to be involved in the work of IRD was George Orwell, the well-known English author and journalist. A supporter of the libertarian left, Orwell was strongly

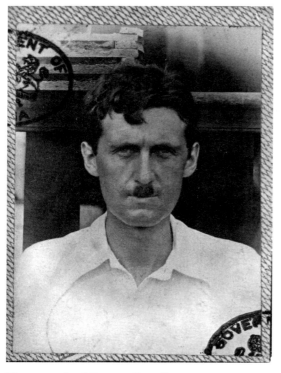

Photograph of George Orwell. *MEPO 38/69*

opposed to Stalinism and became a staunch critic of the Soviet Union. His novels *Animal Farm* and *Nineteen Eighty-Four*, published in 1945 and 1949 respectively, were thinly disguised attacks on Soviet communism and the dehumanising nature of the authoritarian state. Orwell was also the first writer to use the term 'cold war' to describe the post war relationship between Russia and the West. This was contained in a short essay, 'You and the Atom Bomb', published in the magazine *Tribune* in October 1945. Orwell's books soon came to the attention of IRD who funded a series of foreign language versions in Burmese, Chinese, and Arabic and distributed copies to dissident groups in Eastern Europe. The CIA was also involved and subsidised the animated version of *Animal Farm*. Shortly before his death in 1949, Orwell gave IRD a list of writers and journalists he considered to be crypto-communists or fellow travellers and unsuitable to be involved in anti-communist propaganda. The list included well-known names including the novelist J.B. Priestley, the journalist and editor of the *New Statesman* Kingsley Martin and the actor Michael Redgrave.

Cold War fears were reflected in a variety of novels and films. The most influential were:

From Russia, With Love by the British writer Ian Fleming published in 1957 which features his fictional British Secret Service agent James Bond. The story involves a plot by SMERSH, the Soviet counter-intelligence agency, to assassinate Bond and discredit both him and British intelligence. The book plays on the Cold War tensions between East and West, and the decline of British power and influence following the Suez crisis and the demise of its colonial possessions. The novel was later made into a film starring Sean Connery.

On the Beach is a 1957 post-apocalyptic novel set in Australia written by British author Nevil Shute. The book depicts the devastating consequences of a nuclear war in which the Northern hemisphere becomes uninhabitable due to radioactive fallout.

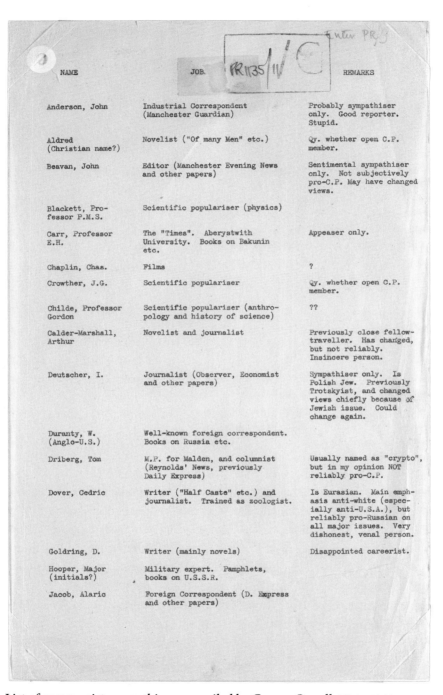

NAME	JOB.	REMARKS
Anderson, John	Industrial Correspondent (Manchester Guardian)	Probably sympathiser only. Good reporter. Stupid.
Aldred (Christian name?)	Novelist ("Of many Men" etc.)	Qy. whether open C.P. member.
Beavan, John	Editor (Manchester Evening News and other papers)	Sentimental sympathiser only. Not subjectively pro-C.P. May have changed views.
Blackett, Professor P.M.S.	Scientific populariser (physics)	
Carr, Professor E.H.	The "Times". Aberystwith University. Books on Bakunin etc.	Appeaser only.
Chaplin, Chas.	Films	?
Crowther, J.G.	Scientific populariser	Qy. whether open C.P. member.
Childe, Professor Gordon	Scientific populariser (anthropology and history of science)	??
Calder-Marshall, Arthur	Novelist and journalist	Previously close fellow-traveller. Has changed, but not reliably. Insincere person.
Deutscher, I.	Journalist (Observer, Economist and other papers)	Sympathiser only. Is Polish Jew. Previously Trotskyist, and changed views chiefly because of Jewish issue. Could change again.
Duranty, W. (Anglo-U.S.)	Well-known foreign correspondent. Books on Russia etc.	
Driberg, Tom	M.P. for Malden, and columnist (Reynolds' News, previously Daily Express)	Usually named as "crypto", but in my opinion NOT reliably pro-C.P.
Dover, Cedric	Writer ("Half Caste" etc.) and journalist. Trained as zoologist.	Is Eurasian. Main emphasis anti-white (especially anti-U.S.A.), but reliably pro-Russian on all major issues. Very dishonest, venal person.
Goldring, D.	Writer (mainly novels)	Disappointed careerist.
Hooper, Major (initials?)	Military expert. Pamphlets, books on U.S.S.R.	
Jacob, Alaric	Foreign Correspondent (D. Express and other papers)	

List of communist sympathisers compiled by George Orwell. *FO 1110/189*

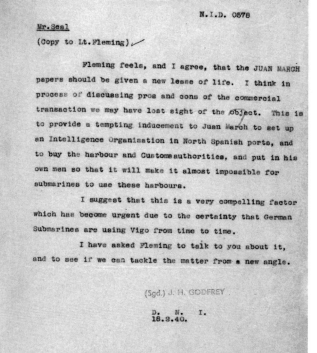

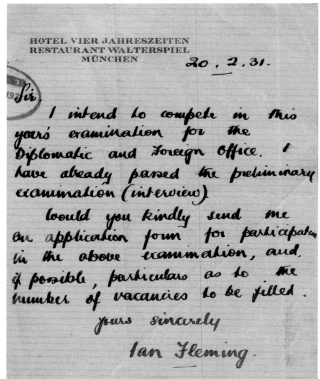

Above left: **Letter from Director of Naval Intelligence to Ian Fleming.** *ADM 223/490*

Above right: **Request by Ian Fleming for an application form to join the British Diplomatic Service, 20 February 1931.** *CSC 11/98*

The only areas of the planet that are not affected are Australia and New Zealand. The Australian government detect a garbled Morse code signal coming from the US city of Seattle and dispatch a submarine to investigate. After sailing along the deserted west coast of America the crew discover that the enigmatic radio signal is due to a broken window frame striking a telegraph key when blown open by the wind. The submarine returns to Australia to discover that the radioactive cloud is heading for the Southern hemisphere. The population have six months left to live with many taking the decision to commit suicide. The book was one of the first to portray the harrowing effects of nuclear conflict and has been described as the most evocative novel on the aftermath of a nuclear war.

Our Man in Havana is a black comedy set in Cuba written in 1958 by the British author Graham Greene. The novel recounts the exploits of James Wormold, a vacuum cleaner salesman, who is approached by British intelligence to become an agent in exchange for money. He accepts the role and, as he has nothing to report, soon begins to fabricate stories to justify his fee. Written before the Cuban missile crisis, the book contains various fictitious reports of unusual military installations hidden in the mountains. The reports are believed by British intelligence, with Wormold the target of an assassination attempt by a foreign power. The book echoes Greene's own experience of working in MI6 during the Second World War where he learnt about the exploits of agent Garbo, a Spanish double agent who provided his German handlers with fictitious accounts of a German spy ring operating in England which he claimed to control. The book was later made into a film with Alec Guinness in the lead role. Both the book and film highlight the fallibility of intelligence agencies and the disinformation campaigns that were conducted by both sides during the Cold War.

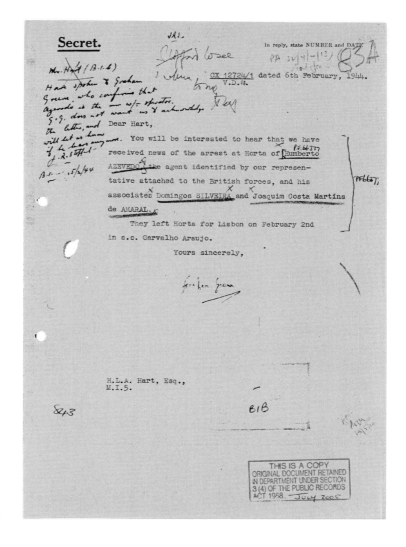

MI6 report signed by Graham Greene. *KV 3/270*

The Manchurian Candidate is a 1959 thriller written by the American novelist Richard Condon. The book details the fate of US Sergeant Raymond Shaw, who is captured during the Korean War. Following his release and return to America, it is revealed that during captivity he had been brainwashed and was now an unwitting assassin for a shadowy Communist conspiracy. Triggered into action by a secret signal, Shaw was programmed to forget his actions once his victim had been killed. In his final mission, he is ordered to assassinate a US presidential candidate so that his running mate, who was a communist sleeper, would be elected. The book was later made into a film starring Frank Sinatra and Janet Leigh and was released in October 1962 as the Cuban missile crisis reached its climax. The subtext of the plot was that communists were infiltrating the United States and that nobody would choose to become a communist of their own free will. It was later revealed that in the 1950s, the CIA had initiated the MK ULTRA program in which scientists had investigated the use of psychedelic drugs, sensory deprivation and hypnosis on human subjects in the search for strange and unusual weapons to employ during the Cold War.

The Spy Who Came in from the Cold is a spy novel by the British writer John le Carré and depicts the heightened tensions that characterized the Cold War in the early 1960s. Published in 1963, the story begins in Berlin shortly after the construction of the wall and involves a British agent, Alec Leamas, who pretends to defect in order to frame a senior East German intelligence officer as a British double agent. The book offers a bleak assessment of the Cold War and questions whether the methods employed by British intelligence are morally consistent with western democracy and values. The political systems of both East and West are characterized by hypocrisy, deceit and indifference to human suffering. The book was later made into a film starring Richard Burton as Alec Leamas and has been described as one of the most emotionally resonant movies ever made during the entire Cold War period.

Dr Strangelove is a 1964 black comedy that plays on Cold War fears of an accidental nuclear conflict taking place between the two superpowers. The film was directed by Stanley Kubrick and stars Peter Sellers and George C. Scott. The story begins with a deranged US air force officer, General Jack D. Ripper, taking control of a bomber base and ordering a nuclear first strike against the Soviet Union. The US President attempts to order the bombers back home but discovers that this cannot be done without first issuing a secret code that only General Ripper possesses. The President telephones the Soviet leader to warn him and is informed that the Russians have invented a doomsday machine that will be triggered automatically should the

SECRET

> PORTON TECHNICAL PAPER NO: 936
> COPY NO: 111
> DATE: 24th August, 1965

A FIELD EXPERIMENT USING LSD25 ON TRAINED TROOPS

by

DIONE J. BERRY, MARY CHEETHAM

SURG. LT. CDR. W.M. HOLLYHOCK, R.N.

FRANCES LOVELL, K.H. KEMP

MILITARY UMPIRE'S REPORT (APPENDIX III)

by

MAJOR J.L. RICKCORD

SUMMARY

The experiment was designed to show what effects a psychotomimetic agent might have on the military effectiveness of men under field conditions.

Before taking part in a simulated anti-terrorist sweep, thirteen Royal Marine Commandos, their officer and two N.C.O.'s were dosed with Lysergic Acid Diethylamide (LSD25). They received 200 µg orally in water, with the exception of one man who was given only 75 µg. Some effects of the drug were observed within 10 mins and within 15 mins the efficiency of the unit was impaired. Military effectiveness continued to decline until the action was terminated 70 mins after exposure, when the men were all incapacitated to some degree, communication between the sections had broken down and the officer had asked to be relieved of his command. In the opinion of the military umpire, if the unit had been facing real opposition it would have been wiped out some time earlier.

SECRET

Porton Down report on the effects of administering LSD to Royal Marine Commandos. *WO 189/444*

country come under nuclear attack. The US army raid the base, retrieve the code and recall the bombers. One of the aircraft has been damaged and does not receive the order to turn back and detonates a hydrogen bomb over a Soviet missile site triggering the doomsday device. Dr Strangelove, the President's wheelchair-bound scientific advisor, declares that the US population could live deep underground in mines untouched by radiation and then re-populate the world once conditions on the surface had improved. In its depiction of events, the film is strongly critical of the concept of mutually assured destruction and raises questions about the effectiveness of US control over its nuclear arsenal. The film has been described it as the best political satire of the century and a harrowing tale of systemic madness.

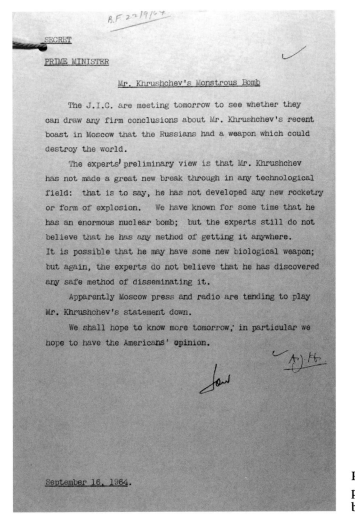

Prime Minister informed of possible Russian doomsday bomb. *PREM 11/5116*

Following the fall of the Berlin Wall, a number of films emerged that depicted life in former East Germany. Two of the most popular were *Good Bye Lenin!* a comedy filmed in 2003 and directed by Wolfgang Becker and *The Lives of Others* released in 2006 and directed by Florian Henckel von Donnersmarck. In *Good Bye Lenin!* the story revolves around Christiane Kerner, an elderly woman who falls into a coma shortly before the fall of the Berlin Wall. A staunch supporter of the East German Communist Party, Christiane awakes from her coma after eight months and is informed that another shock could kill her. Her family are aware that news of recent events would distress her and instead pretend that East Germany is still in robust health. To convince Christiane that all is well, the family dress in their old clothes, restock the kitchen with old East German food and concoct various fake news broadcasts to convince Christiane that all is well. The deception is successful, with Christiane dying peacefully three days after the reunification of Germany. The film shows that, for some, the certainties of the East German state, despite its restrictions, were preferable to the chaos and uncertainty of life in the West.

In contrast, *The Lives of Others* in a stark reminder of the surveillance state operated by the Stasi, the East German secret police. The story begins in 1984, a year chosen deliberately to resonate with Orwell's dystopian novel, and portrays the Stasi investigation into the life of Georg Dreyman a successful East German playwright who falls under suspicion of writing an article critical of East Germany. Dreyman's girlfriend is interrogated and betrays him, later committing suicide. The surveillance is undertaken by Stasi agent Gerd Wiesler, who become increasingly disillusioned with his job and refuses to file reports on Dreyman's activities. He is later demoted and spends the remainder of his career in menial positions. Following the fall of the Berlin Wall, Dreyman consults his Stasi file and realises that Wiesler, referred to in the file as agent HGW XX/7, had concealed his actions from his superiors. He dedicates his next novel 'to agent HGW XX/7, in gratitude'. The film ends with Wiesler passing a book shop and noticing a copy of Dreyman's book in the window. He opens a copy and is deeply moved by the dedication which he sees as a validation of his actions. The film won the 2006 Oscar for Best Foreign Language Film and is widely praised for its factual accuracy and atmosphere evoking the paranoia of the East German state of the late 1980s.

Cold War themes were a staple of many television and radio programmes. These ranged from light hearted adventure series such as *Dick Barton – Special Agent, The Man from UNCLE, Joe 90* and *The Avengers* in which a cast of intrepid heroes battle against a succession of mysterious adversaries, often with Eastern European accents, intent on world domination, to the more challenging post-apocalypse dramas including *The War Game, Threads* and *Survivors*. The world of espionage was also a popular subject for television and radio dramas. Popular examples included *The Traitors* first broadcast by the BBC Light Programme in 1952 and based on the book by Alan Moorhead on the atomic spies Klaus

Fuchs and Allan Nunn May; *Danger Man*, starring Patrick McGoohan, a Washington-based intelligence operative whose missions took him to Africa, Latin America and the Far East; *Tinker, Tailor, Soldier, Spy* starring Alec Guinness as George Smiley who is given the job of unearthing a Russian mole working deep within British intelligence; and *A Question of Attribution*, a screenplay by Alan Bennett based on Anthony Blunt and his role in the Cambridge spy ring and later as art adviser to HM Queen Elizabeth II.

NUCLEAR WARFARE: THREE MAJOR BBC TELEVISION PROGRAMMES

BBC Television is to transmit three important programmes dealing with the likely effects of a nuclear attack on the United Kingdom. They will be broadcast on Sunday 23rd September and Monday 24th September 1984 on BBC-2.

The first programme is a two hour drama documentary based on factual information which covers a 13 year period in the projected life, and death, of the city of Sheffield, during which Britain is devastated by nuclear attacks. The programme is called 'Threads', a reference to the intertwining strands of relationships and resources which support life in a big city.

Its author is the Sheffield writer Barry Hines, who wrote the script for the film 'Kes'. The producer and director is Mick Jackson, who also produced the award winning film 'A Guide to Armageddon' in the BBC's 'Q.E.D.' series.

Actors portraying two Sheffield families and the city's Chief Executive provide the basis for the action. Hundreds of "extras" from the city also take part.

The direct effects of a nuclear blast on the city and its people, and the subsequent long term consequences of nationwide nuclear devastation are depicted in accordance with the research findings of many scientific and professional bodies in Britain, the United States and the USSR.

The evening after the transmission of 'Threads', BBC-2 will show a documentary programme called 'On The 8th Day' produced at Bristol by the BBC Natural History Unit. It takes its title from computer generated maps of the world, which have been used by American and Russian scientists, to predict world temperatures on the eighth day after a nuclear war. Their findings are that, even if only a small proportion of the 55,000 existing nuclear warheads were fired, the whole northern hemisphere would be plunged into a 'nuclear winter', a long twilight with freezing temperatures.

cont....

BBC programmes depicting nuclear attack on the UK.
HO 322/1134

Fear and anxiety about life in the shadow of the bomb inspired many pop artists to produce their most memorable and creative work. Examples include the 1965 hit *Eve of Destruction* by Barry McGuire; *Two Tribes* by Frankie Goes to Hollywood released in 1983 and *The Final Countdown* issued in 1986 by the rock group Europe. In 1990, following the fall of the Berlin Wall, Roger Waters, the co-founder of the rock band Pink Floyd, staged one of the largest rock concerts in history, *The Wall – Live in Berlin*, with an attendance of 450,000. The song *Heroes* by David Bowie tells the story of two lovers from East and West Berlin separated by the Wall. Bowie's performance of the song at the German Reichstag in West Berlin in June 1987, has been considered a cultural catalyst leading to the fall of the Berlin Wall. In January 2016, following his death, the German government acknowledged Bowie's role in bringing down the Wall and for becoming a hero to many modern day Germans.

In addition to films, television and music, the world of sport occupied a highly politicised role during the Cold War, with tensions and rivalries played out on the playing fields and sporting stadiums of East and West. In the early 1970s, the unlikely sport of table tennis was used as a means of improving relations between the People's Republic of China and the United States. The 1971 World Table Tennis Championships held in Japan proved the ideal location. During the tournament, the American and Chinese teams exchanged gifts. This was followed by an invitation authorised by the Chinese leadership for the US table tennis team to visit China. The visit, often referred to as 'ping-pong' diplomacy, was a great success and is credited for reviving diplomatic relations between the two countries. The following year Richard Nixon travelled to Beijing as the first US president to visit communist China.

The Soviets and the Eastern Bloc countries invested heavily in athletics as a means of demonstrating the superiority of their political system. The Olympic Games were often used as a bargaining chip between the two sides and a means of exerting diplomatic pressure. The 1980 Olympic Games in Moscow were boycotted by many western countries following the Soviet invasion of Afghanistan. In response, the 1984 Summer Olympics held in Los Angeles were boycotted by fourteen Eastern Bloc countries, including the Soviet Union and

> **Visit of the President of the United States to China**
>
> *The Foreign and Commonwealth Secretary* said that the visit of the President of the United States to the People's Republic of China appeared to be proceeding satisfactorily and would probably be of considerable assistance to the President in his forthcoming electoral campaign. A second consequence of the visit might be increasing anxiety on the part of the Government of the Soviet Union about Chinese intentions in the short term, particularly if it seemed likely that United States policy towards the People's Republic might become less hostile.

President Nixon's visit to China. *CAB 128/50*

Sussex

PRIME MINISTER'S
PERSONAL MESSAGE
SERIAL No. T130/72

4 April, 1972

Dear Mr. President,

I am grateful to you for your letter of 28 March informing me of your impressions on your return from China.

I was much interested by what you wrote. Your visit must have been both fascinating and important, and I share your hope that the relationship between the United States and the People's Republic of China will continue on the path of peaceful communication which you have initiated.

With warm personal regards.

Yours sincerely,

Edward Heath.

The President of the United States of America

JKS

Prime Minister Edward Heath congratulates President Nixon on his visit to China. *FCO 21/983*

PRIME MINISTER

Chinese Table Tennis Team

The Chinese Table Tennis Team is to visit Britain
between 6 and 19 December. The Chinese Mission in London
have drawn attention to the fact that Chou En-Lai
received the English Table Tennis Team which went to
Peking in April; they have said that they would
welcome a reciprocal gesture.

The FCO advice is that while the Chinese are being
unforthcoming about an exchange of Ambassadors, there
is no necessity for you to receive the Chinese team.
They would, however, raise no objection if you wish
to do so. Alternatively, they have suggested that
you might send a message to the team through
Mr. Griffiths who will be meeting them.

I have asked the FCO to consider whether there is
any way in which the visit of this team might be used
to clinch the exchange of Ambassadors. For example,
by using the occasion to convey a personal message
from you to Chou En-Lai. I will put proposals to
you as soon as I have their reply.

23 November 1971

Prime Minister, Edward Heath, appraised of the political opportunities offered
by a visit of the Chinese table tennis team. *PREM 15/770*

East Germany. To help counter the various boycotts and foster a spirit of cooperation, the Goodwill Games were established. Headed by Ted Turner, the philanthropist and founder of the Cable News Network (CNN), the first games were held in Moscow in 1986 and attracted 3,000 athletes from seventy-nine countries. The Goodwill Games were held every four years with the second event taking place in Seattle in the United States. Following the dissolution of the Soviet Union, the games began to lose public interest and were cancelled, with the last competition taking place in Brisbane, Australia in 2001.

10 DOWNING STREET

THE PRIME MINISTER   16 June 1980

Thank you for your letter of 27 May about British participation in the Olympic Games in Moscow.

It is unfortunate that the Olympic Games happen to be scheduled at this time. I understand and sympathise with the feelings of the athletes who have trained for years with the object of participating. But we know that for the Soviet Union sport is a branch of politics and I would like to draw your attention to the extract from a recent Soviet publication quoted in the attached memorandum. It is clear from this and other evidence that the Soviet authorities will claim participation in the Olympics as endorsement of their aggression in Afghanistan and their propaganda machine will make use of this, both within the Soviet Union and abroad. From this, we have concluded that a boycott of the Olympics by citizens of the Free World would be one of the most effective measures to bring home to the Soviet Government and the Russian people the abhorrence in which their actions in Afghanistan are held. That is why I have advised British sportsmen and women and their sporting federations that it would be against British interests and wrong for them to compete in Moscow.

I see no evidence of antagonism towards athletes by the Government in this. None of the parallels you have drawn can be compared with the unprovoked Soviet invasion of a small and non-aligned neighbour in massive force. Nor were those you criticise hosts for the Olympics. Indeed, never in the history of the modern Olympics has the host country at the time of the Games been committing agression in another country. There is no question of double standards. We believe that it is essential for the future peace

/ of the world

Possible boycott of Olympic Games in Moscow.
PREM 19/376

CHAPTER 8

EVERYTHING CHANGES: AFTER THE COLD WAR

On 9 November 1989, the Berlin Wall, the embodiment of the post war division of Europe, was torn down. Two years later, in December 1991, both the Soviet Union and the Warsaw Pact ceased to exist. Almost overnight, the military threat to western security had disappeared and the Cold War that had dominated international politics for over half a century was consigned to history. Following the collapse of the Soviet Union, the Russian nuclear stockpile decreased by over eighty per cent between 1986 and 2012. The new strategic environment had important ramifications concerning the future role of NATO and western intelligence. New threats soon emerged. The disintegration of Yugoslavia into several breakaway republics resulted in bloody conflicts, leading to a major NATO intervention in Kosovo in 1999. The destruction of the twin towers of the World Trade Centre and the loss of almost 3,000 lives by al-Qaeda in 2001 shocked the world and demonstrated that the threat to international security had changed in ways few people had imagined.

To meet these new threats, NATO was reconceived as a cooperative security alliance working closely with non-NATO countries and other international organizations around the globe in order to achieve security and stability on a regional and global basis. To achieve these objectives and enhance European security, NATO established the Partnership for Peace programme which involved joint military exercises with non-NATO states including the former Soviet republics. To address global concerns, NATO was authorised to act in the defence of 'common interests' rather than 'common territory'. This new mandate paved the way for anti-piracy operations in the Persian Gulf and South-West Africa, the fight against international terrorism and countering the threat posed by weapons of mass destruction.

NATO was not the only organization to experience change. The role and purpose of intelligence agencies was transformed following the end of the Cold War. One immediate consequence was greater transparency. In Britain, the existence of the three intelligence agencies – MI5, MI6 and GCHQ – was belatedly acknowledged by the government and placed on a statutory footing, with Parliament given an oversight role. The adversary may have changed but the techniques and methods developed during the Cold War remain equally valid. The need to disrupt and counter international terrorist networks is now a priority, with resources and staffing levels increased accordingly. The work of the agencies is coordinated to the Joint Terrorism Analysis Centre (JTAC) which works closely with the Counter Terrorism Command of the Metropolitan Police.

Terrorism is not the only new danger facing the West at the start of the twenty-first century. Cyber warfare and computer crime are significant threats to critical infrastructure of the West and for the continued functioning of society and the economy. The degradation of the

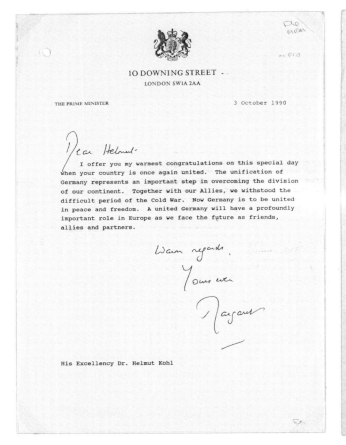

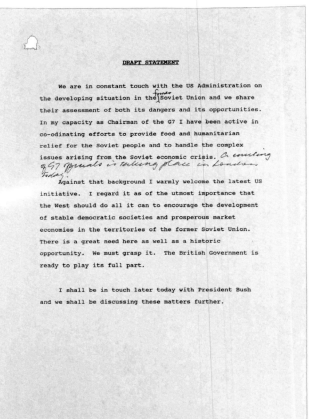

Above left: **Letter from Margaret Thatcher to Helmut Kohl expressing congratulations on German Unification.** *PREM 19/3002*

Above right: **Draft statement by the Prime Minister on developments in the former Soviet Union.** *PREM 19/3562*

environment, climate change, global pandemics and the mass migration of people from the less developed world into Europe and North America pose legitimate security concerns and threats to public order. Russia's military intervention in Georgia and Ukraine has caused some in the West to wonder whether the behaviours and practices inherited from the Soviet Union have really gone away. The rise of China will bring further challenges. The horror of nuclear annihilation may well have receded, but these new threats to security and stability will need to be addressed without a return to the fear and paranoia that characterised the Cold War.

RESTRICTED

FOREIGN AND COMMONWEALTH OFFICE   DD 1992/12
EASTERN DEPARTMENT   DESPATCH
ESC 014/1   GENERAL DISTRIBUTION
                                        RUSSIA
                                        1 JANUARY 1992

RUSSIA: ANNUAL REVIEW FOR 1991
THE RUBBLE OF THE DICTATORSHIP

HER MAJESTY'S AMBASSADOR AT MOSCOW TO THE SECRETARY
OF STATE FOR FOREIGN AND COMMONWEALTH AFFAIRS

SUMMARY

    In 1991 the Communist dictatorship over the Soviet Union
collapsed in ruins, and Russia awoke to find its empire -
one of the most durable and extensive in history - coming to
pieces in its hands. Gorbachev began the year without
friends, and ended it without a job. Yeltsin triumphed, to
face an economic collapse which could bring his reign, too,
to an early end.

JUGAAM/1   RESTRICTED

Foreign Office Annual Report on Russia for 1991: The Rubble of the Dictatorship. *PREM 19/3921*

FURTHER READING

Andrew, Christopher, *The Defence of the Realm: The Authorized History of MI5*, Penguin, London, 2009

Barnett Nicholas J., *Britain's Cold War: Culture, Modernity and the Soviet Threat*, I.B. Tauris, London, 2018

Gaddis, John Lewis, *The Cold War: A New History*, Penguin, London, 2005

Geraghty, T., *BRIXMIS: The Untold Exploits of Britain's Most Daring Cold War Spy Mission*, Harper Collins, London, 1997

Grant, Matthew, *After the Bomb: Civil Defence and Nuclear War in Britain, 1945-68*, Palgrave Macmillan, Basingstoke, 2010

Halliday, Fred, *The Making of the Second Cold War*, Verso, London, 1989

Hilton, Christopher, *The Wall: The People's Story*, Sutton Publishing, Stroud, 2001

Isaacs, Jeremy and Downing, Taylor, *Cold War*, Bantam Press, London, 1998

Mason, John W., *The Cold War 1945 -1991*, Routledge, London, 1996

Taylor Richard, *Against the Bomb: The British Peace Movement 1958 – 1965*, Clarendon Press, Oxford, 1988

Twigge, Stephen, Hampshire, Edward and Macklin, Graham, *British Intelligence: Secret, Spies and Sources*, The National Archives, Kew, 2008

Walker, Martin, *The Cold War and the Making of the Modern World*, Fourth Estate, London, 1993

Westad, Odd Arne, *The Global Cold War: Third World Interventions and the Making of Our Times*, University Press, Cambridge, 2005

INDEX